RH SYSTEMS

In conjunction with Hungerford Town F.C
Would like to congratulate Tony Williams for the fantastic service he has given to promoting the Non - League family for over 5 decades.

RH - 35 years successfully

Working with International manufacturers to help design, install & erect projects on time for a wide customer base

01793 827723   www.rhsystems.co.uk

RH Systems - Office refurbishments
   RH Storage - Shelving & Racking
      RH Air-Conditioning - Daikin D1 Installer

Motor companies, - Honda, Rolls Royce, BMW, Jaguar

Government agencies, - United Nations, U.K Prisons, Local Councils & Charities.

Schools Colleges & Universities

International & Private Companies, - ITW, Siemens, Comau

R+H Storage Ltd
Unit 18, Equity Trade Centre, Hobley Drive
Swindon, Wiltshire, SN3 4NS

Tel 01793 827723
Email sales@rhsystems.co.uk

www.rhsystems.co.uk

Company Reg: Cardiff 4095153

Vat UK: 768337195
R+H Terms & Conditions apply (available on request)

R+H Air Conditioning is a division of R+H Interiors Ltd

Arguably a Love Story

Cover: A Muratti goal against Jersey.

Copyright Tony Williams 2018

All rights reserved.
No part of this publication maybe reproduced, stored in a retrieval system or transmitted in any form or by any means electronic mechanical, photocopying, recording or otherwise, without prior permission in writing from the copyright holder.

Compiled and designed by:
BCF Books   www.bcfbooks.co.uk

Published by   Mike Williams Publishing   T: 01548 531339

Printed and bound by CPI Group (UK) Ltd, Croydon, CR0 4YY

INDEX

1938 - 1958	9
Birmingham	11 & 15
Hallfield School	13
League Tables	16
Malvern College	18
RAF Isle of Man	22
Reading FC Contact	24
RAF + Bedford Town	26
1959 - 1969	29
Corinthian Casuals	30
Reading as a Player	34
Redhill	36
RAF Football	39
Sir Stanley Rous	45
Old Malvernians	46
Channel Islands	50
Epsom & Ewell	58
The Amateur Footballer	60
Jimmy Hill	61
1970 - 1986	65
The Rothmans Years	66
Launch of Football Yearbook	68
Intro 1st League Sponsorship	70
Hungerford Town	78
Somerset Cricket	90
Italian, Wales & Eire Tours	95
1990 -1997	99
Yeovil Years	100
North Curry	109
2000 -2017	111
TW Publications	112
30 Years of Non-League Directory	123
'You Have to Love it' Photos	136
Conclusion	138
Photographers	141
Selection of Covers	142

Introduction to this History

This history is dedicated to the millions who have loved their involvement with Non-League football as players, coaches, managers, club officials, league officials, match officials and supporters. Once the spirit of comradeship and sportsmanship on and off the field has been experienced it is never forgotten.

For some reason I was born with football in my blood. Without seeing a game, I was fascinated by the names of the clubs, fell in love with my first school football kit on sight and apparently kicked a ball about with both feet from the age of five. I was obviously an unusual child!

But luckily, this passion has given me a wonderfully happy life, introduced me to some treasured friends and I am still enjoying my lifelong involvement with the game. Having compiled and published a varied selection of publications, my eldest son Michael, has now taken up the challenge of providing Non-League football information for the public, through web sites as well as publications.

I hope this will turn out to be a Modern History of Non-League Football as we have seen it. I have enjoyed being involved at many different levels but there are so many subjects to feature - new clubs being formed and some disbanded, the varying scale of payment for players, the introduction of promotion and relegation and new pyramid structures of leagues, plus representative and International football and the excitement of FA Cup giant killing. The introduction of The FA Trophy and FA Vase after the disappearance of the 'amateurs' plus the basic changes in football and life itself - all these make a wonderful story, within which I am proud to have played a tiny role and have enjoyed it all.

Not many people can look back at a life in which they have been lucky enough to have enjoyed a variety of happy and uplifting involvement within their chosen sport.

I could hardly have enjoyed myself more. I owe so much to relatives, friends and football people for these treasured memories within the varied levels of Association Football, our national sport, which, for some reason, captured my heart from a very early age.

When I look back and realise how lucky I have been to experience such a happy and contented life, I wanted to acknowledge this happiness and say thank you to many people who seem to have been in the right place at the right time to help me.

Tony Williams

Photo top left:
Being awarded a medal for 'an outstanding contribution to football' at The Grassroots Heroes Reception at Buckingham Palace in October 2015

Thank Yous

To two dedicated and loving parents.........   ....and my sister

My Father and Mother had survived pressure from their parents when they announced they were planning to get married. But these worries had given their relationship extra strength, and I never ever heard a cross or unpleasant word between them.

They were never financially comfortable, but they were determined I should have a good education and when we moved down to Devon after the war, I was accepted by Mount House Preparatory School in Tavistock.

I will always feel extremely grateful for their decision to pay for my private education. But at the time, I didn't realise the importance of their unselfish determination to give me this opportunity. I didn't appreciate the importance of their efforts and looking back, I didn't make the most of my education off the field!

My parents had both enjoyed sport at school and my Father had played senior club Rugby in the West Country after being captain of his school, which had changed codes from Association to Rugby Football while he was a senior student.

My parents' happy, loving atmosphere in the home, despite their financial worries, of which I wasn't aware at the time, gave me a very happy start to life which developed better on the sports field rather than the classroom. They were very special!

Apparently, having seen a school play in which a special youngster called Caroline had been the first little girl I had admired, I was very keen that my newly born baby sister should be called Caroline, and my parents seemed to agree.

The age difference and the fact that I was away so much at boarding school, meant we didn't have time to get fed up with each other, in fact we became good friends which has lasted throughout our adult lives.

Caroline has a grown up family of her own and has enjoyed great success with her artistic ability. This has enabled her to enjoy participating in local arts and crafts in many ways - setting up her own craft gallery; helping to set up and run an arts centre and, more recently, returning to study fine art at University.

I have benefited from her love and support which have never faltered during my ups and downs, and the fact that this book has actually been completed, is thanks to Caroline's patience and artistic publishing skills. I have been very lucky to have had such a very speclal sister.

Thank Yous

Thank you to 'RVR" (Headmaster Rigby) and Football master Eric Boulton.

At the end of four exciting years, developing on and off all the Edgbaston Preparatory School (Hallfield) sporting fields, my parents had decided that considering the situation of our Bentley Heath home and our financial situation, I should continue my education at Solihull Grammar School if they would have me.

But thanks to the influence and driving force of head-master Rigby, I was accepted by Malvern College, and this move became one of the most important of my life. Mr Boulton a young master who had been on Stoke City's books, had supplied my first football coaching and 'RVR' had shown my parents new educational possibilities. The change of plan for my Secondary education proved to be a wonderful move.

Thank you to Harry Johnston who had captained the famous Blackpool side that included Stanley Mathews and Stanley Mortensen and, as a complete surprise, he arrived in Berkshire as the new Reading Manager.

Somewhere in his new office my name and details had been scribbled down on a scrap of paper by the secretary to the previous manager, who I had never met. So it was a nice surprise to be contacted by the famous new Reading boss and even nicer to find that Mr Johnston approved of my potential, signed me on amateur forms and even played me in the Reading A side and the Reserves with the senior professionals

He appreciated I was attending a boarding school and later he appreciated I would be out of reach in the RAF, but he still showed an exciting amount of interest, wrote regularly (long hand - no typing) when I was away, and made me feel wanted and very proud to feel I was on Reading's books, even as an amateur.

Learning the game through Denis Saunders obviously helped and I think my 'Ronnie Allen trick' (foot over the ball) which Mr Johnston noticed in a training five a side, also impressed. But I was proud to be on the books for seven seasons and appreciated the care and interest the Reading manager showed in me. I can only say another very late **'thank you'** for a wonderful experience.

R.V. R

Harry Johnston

Thank Yous

Thank you to Nat Lofthouse of Bolton Wanderers a very important hero who came into my life when I listened to radio commentaries describing the brave battling centre forward play of England's No 9. He scored brave goals for England and I watched him score six for The Football League, including four headed goals, of which three were from his special full length powerful diving headers.

The Inspiration of this wonderful player inspired me to practice heading from all angles and for a 5ft 9 inch striker, I soon realised I could cope with the majority of six foot schoolboy defenders. My first game for the Malvern College First Eleven was, as a 16 year old, away to Wolverhampton Grammar School and I managed three headed goals in a 5-0 victory! I dedicated this special day to 'Sir Nat'! with a "Nat Trick".

I even had the thrill of getting to know the great man, when I was involved with Yeovil Town, and was pleased to find him as charming and modest as I had imagined.

Thanks to Nat Lofthouse a hero who never let me down and was a privilege to know.

Thank you Denis Saunders your dedication to football, your standards and obvious love of the game were appreciated by all who passed through your Malvern College teams.

My school provided me with a chance to play football just about every day in the winter months and the introduction of Denis Saunders as our master in charge was timed perfectly. He had captained the successful FA Amateur Cup Winning side Pegasus and was an educated football fanatic with standards, who obviously loved the game.

A great believer in the 'push and run' style that had been successful for Pegasus, a club who had won two FA Amateur Cup Finals in front of 100,000 at Wembley. Denis taught us to keep possession, by playing the way we were facing, keeping it simple and making the ball do the work!

Sounds easy! In fact once you learnt to believe in the principles it was! We didn't attempt to dribble past the opposition unless we were going for goal. Even players with basic natural ability could pass the ball five or ten yards, so we very rarely lost possession and in three years we didn't lose a match to any other school. It was no coincidence that six of Denis Saunders players were selected for England.

Our coach also had strict principles regarding behaviour which was undoubtedly a benefit to all of us for our future years in the game.

Nat Lofthouse

Denis Saunders

These three pictures of celebrations with F.A. Cups at Wembley feature special people in my football life. Harry Johnston, my kind and helpful manager at Reading, is seen as captain of Blackpool with the FA Cup. My hero, Nat Lofthouse was also a successful FA Cup captain with Bolton Wanderers and Denis Saunders celebrates as skipper of FA Amateur Cup winners Pegasus.

Book tree for TW Publications

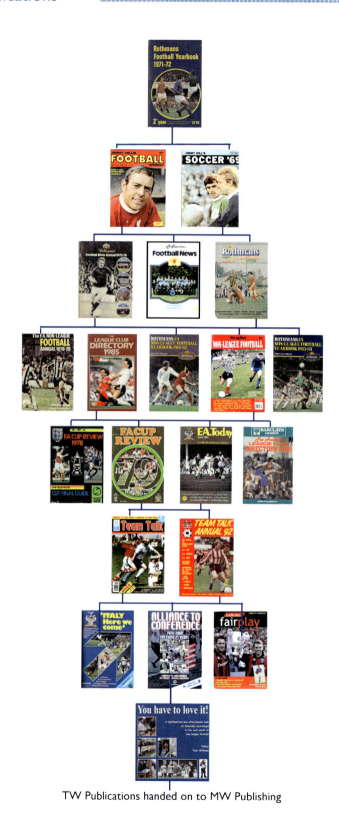

TW Publications handed on to MW Publishing

1938 - 1958

Hallfield Prep School

1938 -1952

During the war my mother and I were billeted out in digs near to my father's different RAF stations. We had rooms at a vicarage near Bristol and it looks as if Mum was encouraging me to practice with my first ball!

West Country Boy

To be born in Bristol in 1938, as Europe was preparing for the Second World War, wasn't great timing. My father, working with the Midland Bank, was to obtain a Secretarial commission in the Royal Air Force and mother was a qualified school teacher.

I was to realise as I grew older that my father's widowed mother resented my mother and the fact that he had left the family home to get married. While my mother had come from a Plymouth Brethren background and changed religion as soon as she was away from her family home. However, they were both very much in love with each other and were delighted to be independent and I enjoyed a very happy childhood.

Once the war started we followed my father around as he was posted all over Britain, but eventually after celebrating 'D' Day in Bristol, we moved to Tavistock where Dad re-joined the Midland Bank.

As both my parents had grown up in the West Country it was a popular move for us all. I remember a Sunday morning in Whitchurch, when a colleague of my father in the Midland Bank, arrived from Plymouth on a bus thinking that their special pools perm which they had worked on together, had won them over thirty thousand pounds. (A formidable amount in those days) I can remember the terrible atmosphere at Sunday lunch, after Dad had reminded him that the extra money they had agreed to spend for four weeks had run out the previous week end!

My father, although he had always preferred Rugby, had been captain of his school football team and encouraged me to go up to the village pitch to see if the older boys would allow me to join in their kick arounds. For someone so nervous about most things, I cannot imagine why I had no worries about joining in with the village lads and appeared to be able to hold my own. I also remember when my mother and I collected my new schools football kit, I insisted on putting it all on when we got home and I wouldn't take it off until Dad had come home and seen me in it.

A sign of the times was the insistence that children went to school whatever the weather, and as a seven year old, I can remember walking for three miles in roads covered in thick snow. In good weather we would kick tennis balls around in the school yard before lessons and we played football most afternoons. I was selected to play for my house team at Mount House Prep School with thirteen year olds and again I cannot understand why this didn't seem to bother me. Apparently football relaxed me completely and I was happy doing something that seemed to come naturally.

Football Pools Coupons had opened up a new world for me as Dad loved working out systems and permutations in the hope of finding eight draws and winning a fortune. I loved the names of the clubs on his coupons as they conjured up a mystical world in which Queens Park Rangers and Preston North End were a bit special and there were plenty of Rovers, Rangers, Citys and Uniteds scattered throughout the fixtures. W.H.U. and W.B.A. were also mystical letters with Hartlepools United and Halifax Town two more favourites.

Football in Birmingham

A career move for my father into the Midland Bank overseas head office in Birmingham meant a very big change in surroundings, from the quiet Devon countryside to the 'Second City' hurly burly of Birmingham. But who would I support? Aston Villa, West Bromwich Albion and Birmingham City were all famous names from the pools coupons.

In the same season that I had seen my first ever League game at Plymouth, Birmingham City had won promotion to the First Division as Champions of Division Two and had only conceded 24 goals in their 42 league games and I liked their colours!

There were some famous names in the Second Division at the time but although Blues obviously had an outstanding defence, inspired by the brilliant Gil Merrick, scoring didn't come easily and with very little team strengthening in the close season, goals proved a rarity at St Andrews.

1938 - 1952

1. Birmingham City match day programme and two team sheets for my visits to St Andrews in 1948-1949

2. 'Plymouth Blues.'
Gordon Astall, Alex Govan and Len Boyd *(left to right)* Birmingham City's three ex-Argyle stars return to play against Plymouth Argyle and my future heroes at Birmingham City seemed to have had a friendly working relationship with the Plymouth club as Neil Dougal had also moved to St Andrews from Devon.

3. Birmingham City 1947-1948
Division 2 Champions
Back row, left to right:
Dave Fairhurst (Trainer), Ken Green, Ted Duckhouse, Gil Merrick, Frank Mitchell and Dennis Jennings.
Front Row:
Jackie Stewart, Neil Dougal, Freddie Harris (Captain), Harry Storer (Manager), Cyril Trigg, Harold Bodle and George Edwards.

1938 - 1952

Good morning Mrs Crump can Clarence come out to play?

Our move to Birmingham from a Devon village was a complete change in culture. We had originally moved to Edgbaston in the heart of the built up area, but soon moved out to Bentley Heath, a village outside Solihull, where our little bungalow faced on to the village sports field. The local boys of all ages played football every day in the holidays but a 'caseball' (our description of a proper football), was needed for our daily game on the village pitch and Clarence Crump was the only lad to own a real football.

Mrs Crump never realised why her Clarence was so popular, but she sent him out every morning with a cap, coat and gloves, so we also had goal posts for our game. I played for every minute available, in any position, whether I was wearing my polo necked jersey dyed green to look like my goal keeping hero Gil Merrick, or an ordinary shirt dyed blue to be a Birmingham goal scorer. I never thought about kicking with my right or left foot, but I know I was really happy playing for hours on end. The village lads of all ages from about nine to sixteen all seemed keen to play. There was an honour concerning 'goals' (was the shot over the coat or was it a goal ? we told the truth!) and the matches sometimes lasted all day. Players had to go home for meal breaks at varying times, but the game continued and finished either when it was dark or if it was bedtime, with a scoreline quite possibly about 36-32!

Bentley Heath Boys did arrange friendlies with neighbouring villages such as Hockley, Chadwick End, Elmdon and Lapworth. Some pitches were without proper goalposts or markings and were occasionally littered with cattle 'droppings' to make falling over a very unpleasant experience.

Some games were played on good pitches however and our most impressive opponents were Silhill Wanderers, an ambitious and well organized club from Solihull. This was a special game as it provided my first press cutting.

The game was reported in the Solihull local paper and we were the surprising winners by 2-1, but the local reporter wrote six solid paragraphs without mentioning a single one of our players. He probably didn't know our names but I knew who had scored the winner!

Junior School's Football

Having arrived from Devon at the age of nine, I had joined a very large prep school for boys in Edgbaston, an affluent district of Birmingham. I had to travel by bus down the Hagley Road and change at Five Ways.

At the first day's assembly, a very frightening Mr Rigby, the headmaster, sorted out the boys for the senior game down to game five for football in the afternoon. We were all asked to volunteer for the level of game for which we could cope, so I and another new boy called Summers, who I was sitting by, volunteered for the third game.

Apparently the standard wasn't great and within a week we were both playing in the senior game with the 13 year olds and found ourselves picked for the School in its first match. We had a very average season and I was originally being played as a midget centre half with Summers, who was much bigger, at full back.

It's Different Today

The highlight of the season for me was when my long clearance bounced over the opposing goalkeeper and apparently I jumped up and down in excitement. At next morning's assembly the frightening Rigby congratulated the team on a rare win, but told me to stand up in front of the school and announced that if there was any further show of emotion after scoring I would not be selected for the school again!

The season finished quietly but it was decided I could be useful as a forward and finished the term playing up front. We played rugby in the Easter term and cricket of course in the summer and I was definitely not yet strong enough for rugby or skillful enough for cricket.

While I was enjoying my education at 'Hallfield', having wonderful fun playing sport practically on a daily basis in term time and travelling around Birmingham watching my heroes in the holidays. I was also in cycling range of Blues training ground at Elmdon so I regularly watched training and acted as a very proud ball boy fetching the balls that had sailed over the hedges

The introduction of Eric Boulton, made a difference to the school's team in the next three years. His coaching and general enthusiasm produced a superb side and in the last year we lost just once (but defeat brought terrible sulking from headmaster and coach alike!). Our record in 1951 was 12 victories, one loss with a goal difference of 78-9 of which I managed to score 45.

Very few privately educated boys played football every day in the holidays, toured the Midlands watching the professionals, including my special 'Blues' at their Elmdon training ground and also enjoyed heading the ball, hopefully, in the same style as Nat Lofthouse!

Our opponents weren't very strong, but our performances persuaded the Headmaster to challenge the Housemaster of No 6 House at Malvern College where many Hallfield boys had continued their education. This proved a very special day as apparently I was in the shop window, and did manage to score the winning goal against boys, some of whom were six foot and who all had broken voices and looked like men to us. Mr Rigby was very pleased indeed with the result!. The goal came from a perfect left wing centre from Richard Pemberton, a Southampton supporter who became a life long friend.

Hallfield Preparatory School

1. My first year in the Hallfield Team 1948
   Back row, left to right:
   Hurdman, Taylor, Shelley, Ecclestone, Finch and Gillot
   Front Row:
   Holland, Reynolds, Samworth, Davies and Williams

2. My last year in the Hallfield 1st XI 1952
   Back Row:
   Crawford, Gray, Hoefield, Butler, Rudge and Walker
   Front Row:
   Gillot, Williams, Summers, Taylor and Pemberton

1938 - 1952

It's different today

After entertainment from the marching Shirley Silver Band, supporters would look towards the tunnel to see the first flash of blue. Then, after the visitors had run on to limited applause, Len Boyd, the Blues captain, would lead his team out to a wonderful roar lifting the roof off the stadium --- not walking out alongside the opponents behind the neutral men in black, creating no excitement whatsoever. Very few people come to see the officials!

This change has deprived the fans of a great moment, as their skipper Len Boyd of Birmingham City shows how it used to be - leading his team on.

Only an ex-referee could have changed this routine!!

Dad suggested I could write to some famous players and ask for their autographs. This caused an upset when an unthinking neighbour pointed out to this excited youngster that one of the autographs he had received was only printed, not authentically signed. I threw it away in disappointment, my mother was furious and our friend didn't get invited in again! Happily I did receive a wonderful signature from the one and only Stanley Matthews which has been treasured to this day.

1938 - 1952

BIRMINGHAM CITY FOOTBALL CLUB LTD.

FOUNDED 1875

St. Andrew's
Birmingham, 9

Dear Anthony
Sorry I have not answered your very nice letter before now, I have been rather busy with the season just starting. Enclosed are a couple of programmes one which our playing staff autographed for you, which I hope will be of use.
　　Maybe it is better for you to have moved away from Birmingham, instead of watching you will be able to play football, which I am sure will be much better for your health, as the move down south will also be for your father.
　　Get yourself a pair of soccer boots and get cracking, who knows Anthony Williams may be a name in football if you keep it up. Good luck, and if you decide to be a forward, good shooting.
Your sincerely
Jeff Hall

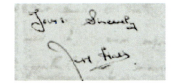

1.
Jeff Hall - was one of the friendliest of the Blues players and I was thrilled when he bothered to reply to my letter. Sadly, after an exciting England career in which he enjoyed a record partnership at full back with Manchester United's Roger Byrne, he died of Polio at the peak of his career.

2. Blues stars after training Ken Green (left) & Gil Merrick

3 & 4.
The day before my first term at Malvern, my father took me to see The Football League play the Irish League at Molyneux. Nat Lofthouse scored six, including four spectacular headers. On the way home we were joined on the station platform by the southern based FA XI players and with only a pencil available I collected some autographs on the programme. The signatures soon disappeared, but I have also kept pictures of the typical Nat Lofthouse headed goals.

1938 - 1952

Football League Tables 1946 - 47

DIVISION 1	P	W	D	L	F	A	Pts
Liverpool	42	25	7	10	84	52	57
Manchester U.	42	22	12	8	95	54	56
Wolverhampton W.	42	25	6	11	98	56	56
Stoke C.	42	24	7	11	90	53	55
Blackpool	42	22	6	14	71	70	50
Sheffield U.	42	21	7	14	89	75	49
Preston N.E.	42	18	11	13	76	74	47
Aston Villa	42	18	9	15	67	53	45
Sunderland	42	18	8	16	65	66	44
Everton	42	17	9	16	62	67	43
Middlesbrough	42	17	8	17	73	68	42
Portsmouth	42	16	9	17	66	60	41
Arsenal	42	16	9	17	72	70	41
Derby Co.	42	18	5	19	73	79	41
Chelsea	42	16	7	19	69	84	39
Grimsby T.	42	13	12	17	61	82	38
Blackburn R.	42	14	8	20	45	53	36
Bolton W.	42	13	8	21	57	69	34
Charlton Ath.	42	11	12	19	57	71	34
Huddersfield	42	13	7	22	53	79	33
Brentford	42	9	7	26	45	88	25
Leeds U.	42	6	6	30	45	90	18

DIVISION 2	P	W	D	L	F	A	Pts
Manchester C.	42	26	10	6	78	35	62
Burnley	42	22	14	6	65	29	58
Birmingham C.	42	25	5	12	74	33	55
Chesterfield	42	18	14	10	58	44	50
Newcastle U.	42	19	10	13	95	62	48
Tottenham H.	42	17	14	11	65	53	48
W.B.A.	42	20	8	14	88	75	48
Coventry C.	42	16	13	13	66	59	45
Leicester C.	42	18	7	17	69	64	43
Barnsley	42	17	8	17	84	86	42
Nottingham F.	42	15	10	17	69	74	40
West Ham U.	42	16	8	18	70	76	40
Luton T.	42	16	7	19	71	73	39
Southampton	42	15	9	18	69	76	39
Fulham	42	15	9	18	63	74	39
Bradford P.A.	42	14	11	17	65	77	39
Bury	42	12	12	18	80	78	36
Millwall	42	14	8	20	56	79	36
Plymouth Arg.	42	14	5	23	79	96	33
Sheffield W.	42	12	8	22	67	88	32
Swansea T.	42	11	7	24	55	83	29
Newport Co.	42	10	3	29	61	133	23

DIVISION 3 (SOUTH)	P	W	D	L	F	A	Pts
Cardiff C.	42	30	6	6	93	30	66
Q.P.R.	42	23	11	8	74	40	57
Bristol C.	42	20	11	11	94	56	51
Swindon T.	42	19	11	12	84	73	49
Walsall	42	17	12	13	74	59	46
Ipswich T.	42	16	14	12	61	53	46
Bournemouth	42	18	8	16	72	54	44
Southend U.	42	17	10	15	71	60	44
Reading	42	16	11	15	83	74	43
Port Vale	42	17	9	16	68	63	43
Torquay U.	42	15	12	15	52	61	42
Notts. Co.	42	15	10	17	63	63	40
Northampton	42	15	10	17	72	75	40
Bristol R.	42	16	8	18	59	69	40
Exeter C.	42	15	9	18	60	69	39
Watford	42	17	5	20	61	76	39
Brighton	42	13	12	17	54	72	38
C. Palace	42	13	11	18	49	62	37
Leyton O.	42	12	8	22	54	75	32
Aldershot	42	10	12	20	48	78	32
Norwich C.	42	10	8	24	64	100	28
Mansfield T.	42	9	10	23	48	96	28

DIVISION 3 (NORTH)	P	W	D	L	F	A	Pts
Doncaster R.	42	33	6	3	123	40	72
Rotherham U.	42	29	6	7	114	53	64
Chester	42	25	6	11	95	51	56
Stockport Co.	42	24	2	16	78	53	50
Bradford C.	42	20	10	12	62	47	50
Rochdale	42	19	10	13	80	64	48
Wrexham	42	17	12	13	65	51	46
Crewe Alex.	42	17	9	16	70	74	43
Barrow	42	17	7	18	54	62	41
Tranmere R.	42	17	7	18	66	77	41
Hull C.	42	16	8	18	49	53	40
Lincoln C.	42	17	5	20	86	87	39
Hartlepools U.	42	15	9	18	64	73	39
Gateshead	42	16	6	20	62	72	38
York C.	42	14	9	19	67	81	37
Carlisle U.	42	14	9	19	70	93	37
Darlington	42	15	6	21	68	80	36
New Brighton	42	14	8	20	57	77	36
Oldham Ath.	42	12	8	22	55	80	32
Accrington S.	42	14	4	24	56	92	32
Southport	42	7	11	24	53	85	25
Halifax T.	42	8	6	28	43	92	22

There were only two points for a victory in those days

When my family had planned the move to the Midlands I obviously knew little about the state of amateur Non-League football, but it's interesting to see the names featured in the League Tables from the forties.

The Isthmian and Athenian Leagues were respected as the senior competitions. Both contained some of the big name clubs in Amateur Football and The England Amateur team was usually selected from them, despite the constant reminders from Northern League giants Bishop Auckland and Crook Town. It's interesting to see which leagues and clubs have survived since those early post war days.

The League tables underline the changes in seniority amongst some famous names. They were comparatively good days for famous Lancashire clubs such as Blackburn Rovers, Blackpool and Bolton Wanderers.

But there is a strangely depressing emphasis on the Northern dominance of this list of clubs who are no longer in The Football League; such as Barrow, Chester, Darlington, Gateshead, Halifax Town, Hartlepools United, New Brighton, Newport County, Southport, Stockport County, Tranmere Rovers, Wrexham, and York City.

Before the introduction of Sponsors linking their names to regional football leagues, The Isthmian and Athenian leagues challenged each other for supremacy in the Home Counties. In the eighties some senior Athenian clubs chose to join the Isthmian League and in 1987 the Athenian League closed down.

Looking at the famous names in the two competitions in 1947-48, its good to see that the modern Isthmian League, known at present as The Bostic Premier Division, still includes Dulwich Hamlet, Enfield, Hendon, Kingstonian and Tooting & Mitcham United who continue to enjoy their traditional rivalry. While famous ex Isthmian clubs such as Wycombe Wanderers and Wimbledon have developed and moved upwards.

The big rivalry In the old FA Amateur Cup was highlighted by The Northern League Clubs, dominated by the famous Bishop Auckland and Crook Town and their Southern counterparts from Isthmian and Athenian Leagues, who produced some wonderful games played in front of impressive attendances.

1938 - 1952

Football Non-League Tables 1947 - 48

NORTHERN LEAGUE

	P.	W.	L.	D.	Goals For	Agst.	Pts.
Ferryhill	26	20	2	4	90	40	44
Bishop Auckland	26	17	6	3	90	41	37
South Bank	26	13	6	7	61	40	33
Shildon	26	15	11	0	52	51	30
Evenwood	26	12	9	5	53	44	29
Stanley	26	10	9	7	60	62	27
Tow Law	26	12	11	3	58	61	27
Crook	26	12	11	3	53	58	27
Willington	26	11	12	3	53	54	25
West Auckland	26	8	13	5	57	73	21
East Tanfield	26	7	14	5	52	67	19
Whitby	26	8	15	3	52	76	19
Heaton Stan.	26	4	15	7	47	66	15
Billingham	26	5	20	1	51	96	11

ISTHMIAN LEAGUE
SENIOR SECTION

	P.	W.	L.	D	Goals For	Agst.	Pts.
Leytonstone	26	19	6	1	87	38	39
Kingstonian	26	16	4	6	74	39	38
Walthamstow Ave.	26	17	6	3	61	37	37
Dulwich Hamlet	26	17	7	2	71	39	36
Wimbledon	26	13	7	6	66	40	32
Romford	26	14	11	1	53	47	29
Oxford City	26	10	11	5	50	68	25
Woking	26	10	13	3	63	55	23
Ilford	26	7	11	8	51	59	22
St. Albans City	26	9	15	2	43	56	20
Wycombe W.	26	7	14	5	51	65	19
Tufnell Park	26	7	15	4	38	83	18
Clapton	26	5	17	4	35	69	14
Corinthian-Cas.	26	5	19	2	33	81	12

ATHENIAN LEAGUE
SENIOR SECTION

	P.	W.	L.	D.	Goals For	Agst.	Pts.
Barnet	26	18	6	2	86	38	38
Hendon	26	14	7	5	45	30	33
Bromley	26	12	8	6	60	50	30
Tooting and M.	26	12	10	4	46	41	28
Wealdstone	26	9	9	8	44	36	26
Enfield	26	10	10	6	55	60	26
Hayes	26	9	10	7	43	43	25
Sutton U.	26	9	10	7	32	38	25
Leyton	26	10	11	5	48	59	25
Finchley	26	10	11	5	38	52	25
Hitchin T.	26	10	12	4	43	61	24
Redhill	26	8	13	5	32	39	21
Barking	26	6	11	9	27	37	21
Southall	26	6	15	5	37	52	17

Malvern College Football with Denis Saunders (1955-56-57-58)

The country had settled down in the much appreciated peacetime spirit. Football was well established as the country's most popular sport with big crowds flocking into stadiums, most of which were dominated by terraces and needed development to improve general comfort.

Thanks to Mr Rigby, my headmaster at Edgbaston Prep School, who arranged for me to successfully apply for a Sports grant at Malvern College, my parents could afford to send me to a football playing public school. The timing was perfect, as Denis Saunders, the captain of Pegasus, the famous Amateur Cup winning club that had twice attracted 100,000 to Wembley, had joined the school and would be in charge of Association Football.

I grew up physically very slowly in my first two years at Malvern and was scared that my sports scholarship would be seen as misplaced, as I showed no outstanding talent with the Colts teams.

Luckily I filled out physically, and Denis Saunders was well settled in charge of the first team at Malvern. My first inter-school match was at Wolverhampton Grammar School as an inside forward encouraged to play in the traditional 'push and run' style, coached by Arthur Rowe so successfully with Pegasus.

The match couldn't have gone much better. I was well prepared having enjoyed the start of the season with Reading in the summer holidays and the game was a dream come true. A hat trick of headers in true Nat Lofthouse style and the first boy to earn his 'colours' after one inter-school match! At least I had justified my scholarship and there were more years to be enjoyed.

In fact we were never beaten by another school in the three seasons and we enjoyed wonderful games against our main rivals Repton and Shrewsbury, and also won the Schools 6-a-side Final, 6-0 against Hulme Grammar School in 1957. Obviously, the Old Malvernians also benefitted as the school began to send a regular flow of talented and well coached footballers for consideration for the Old Boys club, that in itself had an impressive history highlighted by winning The FA Amateur Cup 5-1 v Bishop Auckland in 1902. I was pleased to be invited to attend a schools FA Coaching week at Lilleshall under the guidance of the senior England coach for Amateur football, Norman Creek, and apparently my 'foot over the ball trick' (as taught by Ronnie Allen) caught his eye and I was selected in his 'Team of the Week'!

Denis Saunders coaching had already helped four Malvernians to be selected for the England Under 18 schools annual international against Scotland, and in 1957, Mike Theobald our school skipper and myself were also selected by Norman Creek to face the Scots at Celtic Park. The whole occasion was a wonderful memory, we played well but didn't score. The Scottish keeper was voted man of the match and we conceded three goals in the last few minutes!

The fact that we were booed and jeered at throughout the game, hasn't made me particularly fond of the Scots, but Willie Waddell, the famous ex Glasgow Rangers International, who reported the game for the National Press, gave me a favorable write up as the only English player in his report. So I suppose that was the icing on a memorable and very exciting never to be forgotten experience.

One of the most rewarding aspects of playing for England was the fact that our father had been alive to enjoy the excitement. He had watched me play for Hallfield school in Birmingham and Malvern College in Worcestershire, after travelling across the Midlands in two or three different buses.

Without ever possessing a car, he had originally guided me around Birmingham using the Corporation and National bus routes to watch home games at St Andrews, The Hawthorns and Villa Park. He never grumbled, despite not being fully fit and I hope he really enjoyed our outings as much as I did.

He would even take me to the Birmingham matches very early so we could get a place on a ledge above the gangway half way up the main covered terrace, and I could stand on a step with a clear view. Waiting an hour and a half to kick off was at least livened by The Shirley Silver Band marching and playing. The sound of 'The Standard of St George' signalled their entrance and the band varying marching skills also proved entertaining!

The news that our father had died suddenly, collapsing on the way to work, was given to me by my housemaster at Malvern at the beginning of my last summer term. By luck, a schoolmaster relative from Berkshire was visiting and offered me a lift back to Reading that evening to be with Caroline and our mother who were both amazingly brave.

I was very pleased to read the headmaster's comments in my school report that term.

Headmaster's Report. A.K.Williams.

I should not have thought it possible for a boy to have developed so well. He has made an outstandingly good School Prefect and I am very grateful to him. All who have come into contact with him have spoken to me of his cheerful efficiency and I am extremely sorry to see him go. If it is not an impertinence to say so I am quite sure that he has gained in stature as a person from the time that he had to face personal sorrow I admire him greatly.

D.D.Lindsay

Housemaster's Report.

I have been more than grateful to him for his work in the House this term. He has given real leadership by personal example & I'm not only talking about the football field where he has reigned supreme.

He will be very hard to replace.

J. Farebrother.

Malvern College Football

1. Malvern College 1955
   P7 Won 4 Drawn 3 Lost 0 Goals: For 29 Against 8
   Back row, left to right: Theobald, Williams, Preston-Jones, Walton, Stevens and King.
   Front Row: French, Beeson, MacLaurin, Costeloe and Ellis.

2. Malvern College 1956.
   P7 W7 D0 L0 Goals: F24 A6
   Back row, left to right:
   Bridge, Green, Stevens, Loader and Davies.
   Front Row: Preston-Jones, Walton, French, Theobald, Ellis and Williams.

3. Malvern College 1957
   P7 W4 D3 L0 Goals: F35 A 7
   Back row, left to right: Daniels, Matthieson, Cobb, Heron, Irvine and Styles
   Front Row: Jagger, Williams, Theobald, Preston-Jones and Kennan

4. Malvern College National Schools Six-a-Side Winners 1956
   Goals: F17 A2
   Left to Right:
   David Loader, Peter Ellis, Mike Theobald (Captain), Paul Walton, Tony Williams and David French

Malvern College Football

Many years after I had left Malvern, Denis Saunders apologised to me and admitted I had been picked by Norman Creek for the England Youth team to play an international at Upton Park, West Ham. But as it was during term time, the headmaster had not given permission for me to be involved and I hadn't been told about the selection.

The good side to the sad story is the fact that David Jacobs from Alleyns School played in that game at inside left (back row, third from the left) and this was a very happy turn of events. As, after a lively few years with his University team and Corinthian-Casuals, where we became good friends, David died from cancer in his mid twenties. At least he had enjoyed all aspects of University life and had played for England.

1. A proud moment, walking on for England

3. David Jacobs *(third from left in the back row)* in the FA XI at Upton Park

2. England Under 18s April 1957
   Back row, left to right: McGarry, Norris, Swannell, Hines and Williams
   Sitting: Maltby, Bateson, Theobald (Captain), Luke, Jackson and Rees
   Front: Murphy and Gooding

Malvern College Football

Malvern Misfortune Against Repton

Early Lead lost During Desperate Defence

Malvern 1   Repton 1

Malvern have not been beaten by Repton since 1948, yet on Saturday they could count themselves lucky to have been able to squirm out of Repton's grasp. Malvern, infact, surrendered their lead late in the second half when centre-half Heron, had the misfortune to stumble into a hard centre from Pilkington and divert the ball into his own net.

Repton came to this match having scored 24 goals in their previous four school matches, and it says much for Malvern defense that no Repton forward scored. Malvern were in the lead after three minutes when, from a Williams corner, Styles headed past an unsighted Shentall. The battle was on, Repton surged into attack with their most dangerous moves coming from the left flank. Repton should have equalised when Pilkington received a through ball from Vaughan on the inside of Jagger, but his shot soared over the bar. Malvern now seemed to sense that the ball was running for them, and this feeling must have been reinforced when Vaughan shot from some 10 yards, hit Cobb, the Malvern goalkeeper, in the face knocking him over and as he rose to his knees a second shot swung straight into his hands.

Always a Delight

The second half started at a fast pace. Both centre halves dominated the middle of the field, and neither centre forward was able to break loose. Styles tried both flanks but with the Malvern wing halves defending desperately, they did not have the time to pin-point their passes to him. Phillips, playing in the place of the injured Malvern captain Theobald, was the busiest defender - Vaughan was everywhere, yet Phillips was always in attendance, tackling back again and again. Williams was, however, the hinge to all the Malvern play, and on the day was the best player on the field. Here was an artist whose swerve and intricate footwork were always a delight to watch, and yet he was prepared to tackle back, to fetch and carry. Williams it was who crashed the ball against the Repton cross-bar after 10 minutes in the second half, and minutes later he hurled himself horizontally at a cross from Farrer, but the advancing Shentall intercepted and cleared.

Repton, urged on by their cheering supporters, staged attack. Pilkington looked dangerous, and his centres pitched for the far post were a constant menace, as Edge and Vaughan, tall and jumping high, positioned themselves for the pounce. Yet it was from two lofted crosses from the right that Repton came nearest to scoring. First Jagger bobbed up on the goal-line to head clear with Cobb beaten, and then, with the ball headed in and the Repton supporter's straw hats 30ft in the air, the referee penalised a Repton forward for off-side. Now came the bitter pill for Malvern, as their centre half Heron stabbed the ball past his own goalkeeper as he ran back to cover Pilkington's accurate centre. Malvern now fought desperately for the winning goal, but there was little time left and it was soon over. A match full of excitement and honest endeavour; a feast for all who watched.

1. Malvern College   2. Special Malvern v Repton   Press report from The Times

Isle of Man Football 1958 in the Royal Air Force

A happy return to the Island for a holiday with two great Malvernian friends, Ian Preston-Jones, a very solid centre half and Derby County fan and David Loader a speedy winger, with whom I was to play for seven different clubs before he tragically died with cancer far too young.

National Service was still compulsory for most young men and being in the RAF section of my school Combined Cadet Force, I was offered the chance of an interview with a senior officer in London, to see what I would be best suited for in my two years service after leaving school.

Having a name beginning with a W, I was the last to be interviewed. It was a Wednesday afternoon and in those days FA Cup replays were often televised on midweek afternoons, I was watching the clock as West Ham United v Tottenham Hotspurs kicked off at 2 o'clock and was to be televised.

I was eventually called in and the officer remarked on the fact my records showed I was keen on football, so as he was a West Ham supporter, he suggested we go to the Officer's Mess and watch the game from there.

Well, I couldn't remember any serious questions in any way reflecting my suitability for going directly onto officer training when I joined the Royal Air Force at the end of term. We discussed the game and enjoyed the match, said good bye and apparently I came out top of those being interviewed and would go straight to The Isle of Man for Officer Training after Christmas. As I was on Reading's books, Mr Colvin the station Clerk of Works at RAF Jurby, who was on the Peel Football Club committee, suggested I might like to play for them while on the Island.

As I had realised that football had helped me gain entry to Malvern College and successfully achieving a place on The RAF Officer Training Course, I soon had no doubt that football was also influential in The Services, where everyone seemed to take sport very seriously. Being a fit nineteen year old, it wasn't surprising that I managed 24 goals in 10 games for Peel and I was proud to play for The Island, help my club win The Island's League Championship and FA Cup and thoroughly enjoyed winning the Island 5-a-side tournament with RAF Jurby. Great memories so soon after leaving school.

As the youngest on the course I was pleased to be around mid table in exam results. So was surprised when the RAF officers in charge told me I was being given a re-course and should stay for another twelve weeks, but not to worry, as I wouldn't be put under any pressure!

This was strange, as we had all been under severe daily pressure for the whole of the initial course and were trying desperately to prove we were officer material. It was then pointed out to me that the station football team were soon to be traveling to RAF Uxbridge for the Group Championship, while Peel had the Island FA Cup Final to play. I was now going to be available for selection for both!

My re-course brought me in touch with some special friends, Ray Greenall and Norman Jennings, both older than me and experienced Non-League footballers from the Midlands, who were in my new training squadron. They taught me how to look after myself on the field and also how to gain a little more success socially!

I realised as an officer cadet, my standing amongst the young girls at the Saturday evening dances was encouraging, and I especially remember The Majestic Hotel's Saturday dances, where all the tables around the dance floor had phones, from which we could contact each other around the room.

I plucked up courage to invite a beautiful dark haired youngster to dance and found out she was Ann Corrin the Beauty Queen of Peel, the town that I was scoring goals for every Saturday. It seemed the perfect match and indeed we enjoyed the rest of my stay on the Island.

I was also pleased to be picked for the Island Representative side's 3-3 draw against Liverpool Collegiate Old Boys. The Island team was not very strong, as our RAF XI beat them 2-0 in a charity game in which I met Brian Wakefield for the first time when he was guesting for us in goal.

Peel were the favourites for the Cup Final against Ramsey, but I knew I really wasn't fully fit to play and was very relieved when we won 3-1 and I had managed a couple of goals. The fanatical support from Peel was impressive, it seemed as if the whole town was at The Douglas Bowl and I had really enjoyed a wonderful half a season with a great club.

I have some wonderful memories of the Isle of Man, and enjoyed my first taste of adult life away from school. The football, the dances, the TT race week and the comradeship with some older friends. So it wasn't surprising that some Old Malvernian friends returned to the Island for an Easter Football tour.

Isle of Man Football 1958 in the Royal Air Force

1. I was lucky to have been invited to join Peel FC, who became Island Champions and Cup winners in a thrilling season

3. RAF Jurby qualified to represent the Island Five a-Side tournament and the team (in white) beat Union Mills in the Final.

5. The beautiful Peel coastline on the West of the Island

2. The Isle of Man senior representative side drew 3-3 with Liverpool Collegiate Old Boys.
   Left to right: Platts, Hawke, Caine, Vincent, Judge, Colquitt, Dale Williams, Mackie, Roskams and Birch

4. Not exactly a good FA Cup Final action picture, but at least it proved that the two of us were playing!

In contact with Reading F.C.

A new scheme had been introduced in the fifties to link senior football playing schools with a local professional Football League club and Malvern College had been linked with West Bromwich Albion. Within this agreement, Ronnie Allen, Albion's England international striker, visited us once a week and proved a great success. I practiced and practiced his special foot over the ball trick and found it certainly worked in the school games.

At the end of term, in his last visit, the famous striker suggested that when we returned home we should all knock on the door of our local professional club, saying we had been recommended by West Bromwich Albion.

What a thought ! Reading were a good Third Division South club, but would they be interested in a youngster who would still be going off to a boarding school in the middle of the football season? Even if I was considered good enough to interest them, I would not be able to earn much and my parents had sacrificed all sorts of things to keep me at Malvern.

Football League professionals were paid a maximum wage of £20 a week but the best amateurs in Non-League football were often offered financial incentives to change clubs. Semi-professionals in leagues outside the Football League, such as the Southern League, often received more than their full time counterparts. But it wasn't about money- what an honour it would be to wear the blue and white hoops of my local club .

The 1954-55 season was drawing to a close, and the school's Easter holidays gave me a chance, if I was brave enough, to visit the club. An early afternoon visit took me into a deserted entrance hall at Elm Park. Ladies voices and the clink of glasses made me think it was a bad time to knock on the Secretary's door.

However, a tentative knock was answered and I nervously explained why I was there. I was asked to leave my name and address by a chap with a glass in his hand and 'thanks for coming, we'll let you know!'

Reading 1955-1961

In the summer, after my visit to Elm Park, Harry Johnston, the famous Blackpool Captain and England International, was appointed manager of Reading and he must have found a note with my name and address in his office, as I received a postal invitation to attend training with Reading's young amateurs.

I was obviously excited and very nervous, but the manager and his coach Bobby Campbell, the ex Scotland and Chelsea forward appeared to think I was worth an Under 18 team place, and in my first game wearing the hoops I scored our first goal. The fact that our goalkeeper came out of goal and scored 4 and we won 26-2 against the local Remand home, put my two goals in perspective, but at least I had played in the Reading colours.

Harry Johnston, the ex Blackpool and England player, and Scottish International Bobby Campbell his assistant, were really great to play for at Reading and although they knew I was regularly going away to boarding school, and then probably National Service, they always encouraged me and made me welcome at Elm Park. I have kept and treasured the regular letters, written by hand from the manager which kept me in touch with Reading Football Club while I was away. Fancy him bothering!

Paddy Slavin and Harry Knott were in charge of the junior sides and to be fair, they were loyal club enthusiasts. but didn't talk as much sense as Denis Saunders. Mid week training was usually organised by Bobby Campbell, and it was always exciting when we played five a sides with the senior professionals, but there was an awful lot of running round the track followed by sprints. Lunch for the lads would be a snack in a local cafe followed by a trip to the snooker club or local cinema. But to be recognised as a 'Reading player' in the town or on the bus or train, was a bit special even if I was just an amateur!

My first Football Combination game was at home against Cardiff City in 1957. In the week I had been staying up in London and had been driven down by a friend to see Reading play at Colchester. We stopped for a snack at a Service station where the Reading coach had already stopped and Manager Johnston kindly offered to leave us two tickets.

Next day my mother phoned to say we had received a telegram asking me to look in for training on Thursday evening, as I was selected for the Reserves on Saturday. I contacted the club, as I was away from home so couldn't train, would I still be playing on Saturday?

I was still wanted apparently, so a very nervous young amateur turned up an hour before kick off on Saturday afternoon only to hear a supporter looking at his programme outside the ground and declaring 'If Tony Williams is inside left I'm not going in!'

That was soon forgotten in the excitement of taking my place in the dressing room and listening to the pre match advice, joining

In contact with Reading F.C.

in the exercises (players didn't go out to warm up before a game in those days) and getting plenty of good wishes from the lads.

We lost the game 1-2 and a few years later I met the Cardiff City centre half Ross Menzies who became a great friend of mine in the RAF Officers team. He was serving in Wales on his National Service at the time and was on Glasgow Rangers books when at home.

On Saturday I was surprised to be picked again. The game was very basic, but this time I was playing on the left wing (Coach Bobby Campbell was convinced I was left footed) I wasn't involved very much and I was faced by a very experienced tough looking full back. However, I did have a chance to test my centering from a left wing corner, with my right foot. The first one was dipping under the bar when the keeper tipped it over, so I hit the second kick a bit harder and it went a little further, before being saved again. At the third attempt I managed to score direct from the corner and I had opened my account for Reading, albeit in a very strange way.

Unfortunately this game brought me a very nasty tackle from the right back and for the first time in my playing career I left the field for patching up. There were no substitutes of course and the kick on the shin blew up with fluid on the bone, so kept me away from work and playing for a couple of weeks - but I had scored for Reading!

1. Slipper Cottage near Reading home during the 50's

2. The injury sustained against Northampton kept me off work for a few days and I seem to have pioneered the beard craze about fifty years too soon?

3. Selection Telegram

4. First Goal for Reading Reserves-from a corner kick ! (The scorer is arrowed)

Football in The Royal Airforce 1958 - 1959 and with Bedford Town

Best man for Ray Greenhall, who taught me a few basics for social life in the Services!

Considering football had been instrumental in gaining me a place on an Officer Training Course, plus an extension to my time on the Isle of Man, it wasn't surprising that I found the services very much influenced by all major sports.

National Service was soon to be cancelled, but we were in the RAF and apparently we should all be counting the days until we could get back to civvy street - what rubbish! On reflection, I learnt that the two years in The RAF, if used properly, could be a great experience in which young men could grow up and learn a lot about life and themselves, before settling down to a career and possibly marriage.

My first job as a National Service junior officer was to welcome the new recruits to the Royal Air Force and with bibles in their right hands, swear them in to be loyal to Queen and Country during their Royal Air Force service. This was not the most exciting, testing or stimulating job and it was hardly uplifting to confront a stream of nervous young recruits, most of whom were away from home for the first time.

A few well known footballers were still reporting for the last year of national service and of course the sports officers attempted to snap them up for their respective teams. One that we managed to get to play for us on his way through was the famous Coventry City character George Curtis.

Bedford was the nearest town and it was not quite near enough to get to Reading for training, so Mr Johnston passed me on to The Bedford Manager Tim Kelly, who was to lead 'The Eagles' to the Southern League Championship and of course they had enjoyed two very famous FA Cup ties with Arsenal in 1955-56. I was offered a game in the Reserves at Luton Town in the Metropolitan League and managed two goals in a 4-3 victory. My boss at Cardington was a keen sportsman so encouraged me to run the station's football teams and play as much as I could for civilian clubs.

As a teenager when first qualifying as a Royal Air Force Officer I was obviously aware I was younger than most of the people with whom I was working. For example, some of the senior NCOs in the department were old enough to be my father and of course had experienced years of RAF service. Luckily Mr Dutton, our senior Warrant Officer, was also a keen football man, who helped run the station team. He made it his job to keep an eye on me and step in with a quiet word of advice if he thought I was struggling.

I dreaded my days on duty as The Station Orderly Officer and remember struggling to cope with a minor fire, a domestic row, a punch up between service men and civilians and a car crash, but not all at the same time!

There were very few single people living in the Officers Mess so we welcomed invitations from the more friendly families living in married quarters and it was the station padre who invited me to meet his daughter Susan, who I invited to the Summer Ball. As very inexperienced RAF drinkers we were invited to early cocktails at an ex-pilots house. He thought it extremely amusing to get the young ones merry before moving on to the Ball.

Needless to say the drinks caught up with me and I disappeared to the gents, where an hour later one of our party found me still feeling ill. Apparently Susan had suffered the same problem and I suppose we just had to put it down to inexperience, but we felt extremely foolish.

I missed the excellent social life I had enjoyed with my colleagues on the Isle of Man, so made the most of a local Bedford Jazz club, the blossoming Professional Wrestling circuit and of course Bedford Town Football club at their impressive ground The Eyrie.

I had kept in touch with the friends made during the officer training course and Ray Greenall had invited me to be best man at his wedding in Leamington. I considered this a great honour but realised it was another occasion at which sensible drinking was imperative. Luckily, despite a dangerous outing with Ray on the Friday night, I managed to complete my duties without too much trouble.

Guernsey man Len Duquemin, a famous goalscorer with Tottenham Hotspur, had moved down to Southern League Football while still a relatively young striker, in those days the Southern League clubs were not bound by a £20 a week wage limit. It was a pleasure to play alongside him and it was kind of Bedford to let me continue training at Eyrie Stadium after Ronnie Rooke had taken over as manager.

The new manager was a famous ex-Arsenal centre forward, who was still keen to play in the training games. However, the

Football in The Royal Airforce 1958 - 1959 + Bedford Town

majority of senior semi-pros in the squad disapproved of the manager using up a place in the first team at his mature age! Consequently, when I was selected for the first team to play in a midweek evening cup-tie at Kings Lynn, alongside the manager, no one was talking to me on the coach or at our pre match snack.

One of the senior players did mention that they hadn't approved of the fact that I passed to the manager in our training five-a-sides and also I shouldn't have been picked as I was an amateur keeping a semi-pro out of the team. I was obviously still learning about the politics of Non-League football!

The social life of commissioned RAF officers could be very hectic and enjoyable and there's no doubt that unless one could train regularly and conscientiously, fitness standards would drop. Sadly, this was a fact that I certainly didn't cope with successfully.

During my National Service I was remembered by Norman Creek, the Schools Manager who was also the England Amateur Team Manager and I felt honoured when selected as Reserve for the FA XI v Oxford University, and inside forward for FA XI's v The Royal Navy at Portsmouth and v London University at Motspur Park. Mr Creek always stressed that these games were trials for the full England Amateur International side, but I knew my all round fitness was deteriorating.

In the London University game the other inside forward was an R.Hunt from the Army who was to become a national hero as the Liverpool and England goalscoring star Roger Hunt, who I am pleased to say has remained a good friend to this day.

Freedom of Bedford Parade and march through the Town

Football in The Royal Airforce 1958 - 1959 + Bedford Town

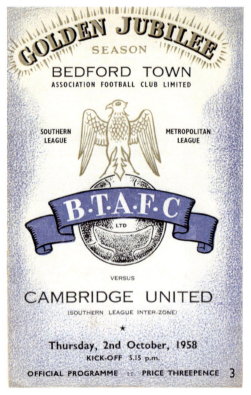

1. Roger Hunt in our FA XI match against London University
2. George Curtis in the RAF Cup winning side
3. A Bedford Town match programme
4. At an RAF Ball with Susan the daughter of our RAF Padre at Cardington

1959 -1969

RAF Innsworth local cup winners

Corinthian-Casuals 1959 - 1964

Holiday work with school teaching colleague Derek Adams

I had promised to play for Corinthian-Casuals after I had left Malvern. They were a club similar to Pegasus but very much involved with competitive Isthmian League Football, playing their home games at The Kennington Oval once the cricket had finished.

Their players were recruited from the senior secondary schools that played Association Football and from the Universities. With players traveling from all over the country and many involved in teaching jobs, coach Doug Flack had a frustrating time trying to get his players to attend training all together,

The club had been formed when the famous Corinthians and Casuals FC, two clubs well supported by old boys clubs and universities, merged to challenge the senior amateur clubs in the home counties, where the Isthmian and Athenian leagues attracted the top teams and best players

I had played a few games for the junior sides but made my first team debut at Barking in the Isthmian League at the beginning of the 1959-1960 season. Also playing his first game was brilliant goalkeeper Brian Wakefield whom I had met when playing in the Isle of Man for RAF Jurby against a touring side.

The game was reported in The Daily Telegraph by Norman Ackland and in the News Chronicle by Panglos, apparently the same chap, who certainly gave amateur football great coverage. I was happy to get the publicity for my two headed goals in a 4-1 victory but was described as an Old Reptonian in the Telegraph!

I was fit and happy and scored 8 of our 25 goals in our first 7 fixtures. Corinthian-Casuals had enjoyed their best start to a season for many years but I broke a toe at Dulwich and never produced the same form in the second half of the season.

After completing my National Service I had accepted the offer from the fearsome Mr Rigby to coach football and do a little teaching back at Hallfield, my old preparatory school in Birmingham. This kept me fit and I enjoyed the coaching just about every day, although I did miss a few Isthmian fixtures when our school matches clashed. However, the headmaster seemed pleased to have a member of his staff playing in the Isthmian League, so time off was usually granted.

In the school holidays I joined teaching colleague Derek Adams in some gardening and odd jobs in the London area and relaxed after the pressures of teaching! Derek was a typical small man who never stopped talking, laughing and generally being a tremendous life and soul of any party. He had a girl friend in London and as I was trying to attend as much pre season training as possible with Casuals in South London, this extra holiday work suited us both ideally.

The 1960-1961 season turned out to be my best in senior football although the Corinthian-Casuals players never trained together and the team changed nearly every week.

Ex- Fulham goalkeeper Doug Flack did a great job as coach in the circumstances and we all made the most of the reunion each week! I really enjoyed playing alongside Robin Trimby an England Amateur international, who was teaching in Shrewsbury, and with his help I managed to score in 21 of the 32 games and finished the season with 28 goals.

One of the outstanding players in the Isthmian League was Paddy Hastie, an Irish striker at Tooting & Mitcham who had played for Aldershot in the Football league as an amateur but had given his Isthmian club terrific service. As luck would have it, Corinthan-Casuals were the opposition when the ace goalscorer was due to play his last match .

We started the 1960-1961 season before the Great Britain football squad had returned from The Olympic Games. So, as Brian Wakefield had been selected as reserve to goalkeeper Mike Pinner for Britain, Corinthian Casuals had promoted my old schoolboy colleague John Swannell into the first team and after the first four matches, this was how the top of the Isthmian League looked! Old school friend David Loader had also started the season in the first team and Old Malvernians had scored seven of the first nine goals.

	P	W	D	L	F	A	P
Corinthian-Casuals	4	4	0	0	9	0	8
Dulwich Hamlet	4	4	0	0	12	6	8
Walthamstow Avenue	5	4	0	1	14	8	8
Bromley	3	3	0	0	17	5	6
Tooting & Mitcham Utd	4	3	0	1	13	4	6

Corinthian-Casuals 1959 - 1962

Star centre forward Paddy Hastie (cartoon artist) played his last game for Tooting & Mitcham United against Corinthian Casuals.

Corinthian-Casuals 1959 - 1962

Corinthian-Casuals players were scattered all over the country so their poor coach really couldn't be expected to prepare his squads for the week-end matches. They met on match days and improvised as well as possible, there were no under the counter expenses so it was not likely that top quality players would choose to play with a team that probably would struggle at the foot of The Isthmian League.

But it was the Isthmian League and it was top class amateur football which was appealing. I was keen to repay the club's officials who had kindly welcomed me back, but after seven games I hadn't scored, although we had won three of the matches.

I had passed the FA Coaching course at RAF St Athans in the summer, so I had taken my first step towards a coaching career so perhaps I should give up playing if I wasn't really fully fit.

At last I managed a goal against Maidstone United and hoped my traditional luck against Kingstonian would last in the next home game. Luckily it did, and I was pleased to score two past Brian Wakefield, but K's had the last laugh winning 4-2.

This was to be my last attempt at coping with the traveling and keeping fit, while also enjoying the social life in the officers mess. I realised I wasn't really worth a place in Isthmian football despite a four goal scoring run before accepting that a very poor performance in a cup tie at Walton & Hersham was just not good enough.

So for the second time I left The Casuals, and would concentrate on football in the Services with a few Old Malvernian cup ties at week-ends which included a losing AFA Senior Cup Final at Dulwich. The Inter Command tournament showed that Tech Training Command were a lot stronger than Maintenance Command. It was good to be playing with Ross Menzies again and I was thrilled to be selected for the Royal Air Force squad for the rest of the season but would be looking out for the chance to do some coaching.

At Christmas, I travelled over to Guernsey where my mother had moved to look after Leonard, her widowed brother. He had lived on the Island through the wartime occupation and a friend suggested I might like to play for his local club's second team in the Christmas holiday challenge against their First Team. St Martins were the Island Champions, and I thoroughly enjoyed the game, scoring in a 4-4 draw and was impressed with the playing surface, the quality of the football and especially the post match celebrations.

The Royal Air Force was not successful in The Inter Service Championship and I was dropped after a disappointing performance in a 2-4 defeat at Portsmouth. However, Icarus had won the Argonaut Trophy against Lloyds Association at Highbury, the touring Icarus squad had a wonderful time in Germany and the full RAF side enjoyed fixtures in Malta and Gibralter. An enjoyable, successful and very social military football season!

1. The excellent Corinthian Casuals 1960-1961 team while I was on duty at Hallfield.
Back row, Geoff Hewitson, Reg Vowells, David Harrison, Brian Wakefield, Mike Smith and Martin Black.
Front Row: John Jessop, Robin Trimby, Joe Bateson, David Jacobs and Pat Neil

2. The Hallfied School Team that I enjoyed coaching ten years after wearing the red and green colours myself.

Corinthian-Casuals 1959 - 1962

1. The best attendance I can remember at a Corinthian-Casuals training session.

2. The Clapton goalkeeper tips over a close range header which really should have hit the target at the Kennington Oval

3. Coach Doug Flack talking to :
Left to right: David Jacobs, Chris Turnbull, Chris Joy, Tony Williams, John Jessop and Robin Trimby.

4. Corinthian-Casuals 1963-1964
Back row, left to right:
Coach Flack, Richardson, Saxby, Clyde, Milton, Joy and Pratt.
Front Row: Harper, Clark, Williams, Jacobs and Critchley.

5. Excellent strike partner, amateur international Robin Trimby in a match against Tooting & Mitcham United at Dulwich

Reading as a Player 1961 - 1962

Harry Johnston obviously had faith in me and my game against Scotland had helped. After disappearing through the RAF training months, I was posted to Andover as a junior officer and in the 1961-62 campaign I was selected for seven matches with Reading Reserves.

I do remember training at Elm Park in an FA Cup week and was surprised by the extra publicity for the Club in the local papers and photographers popping up all over the place for special features. A good cup run was really important to everyone at the Reading club and the fans gave the cup ties great support.

Keeping in touch with Reading was difficult, I had failed a driving test which meant I really shouldn't be driving across to Reading in my little Morris Minor, and secondly, as Officer in charge of football at Maintenance Command Headquarters, I sometimes had to play with the station team before dashing to join Reading for their Wednesday evening Football Combination matches.

The season had been thrilling for me including a trip to St Andrews to play Gil Merrick's Birmingham City Reserves which included Johnny Watts one of my special 'Blues'.

What a day, I even helped the coach driver find St Andrews through the back streets! Walking out on the pitch and looking up to the spot where my father and I used to stand I remembered the times that we had arrived early to get a special place above the alley way. To actually meet Gil Merrick in the corridor, who was now the Blues manager, was very special and he said he would keep an eye on me - he needn't have bothered. I can't remember achieving anything positive, but I was playing centre forward with four wingers making up the front line! To be inside St Andrews changing rooms and to play at the ground that had meant so much to me, was never to be forgotten despite the 2-0 defeat.

I made some good friends at Reading and particularly enjoyed playing alongside Douggie Webb, a local tearaway striker who never stopped running and over a long career scored 100 first team goals. My best game was playing alongside him against Southampton when we both scored special goals, in a fine 2-1 victory.

I kept in touch with Douggie and his wife Joan ever since, as well as David Bridger, a young centre half who was to become an extremely successful business man with his company, Kingsmead Construction Limited, and David Johnston, Harry's son who despite having spent some teenage years with a leg in a splint had represented Chelsea Youth team and played cricket for Berkshire.

Harry Johnston had always stressed that once I could settle down to proper training he would like me to consider turning professional. But having been lucky enough to have enjoyed a good education, for which my parents had sacrificed a lot, the idea of signing for Reading as a professional was exciting but not really sensible. By the time I had finished my national service I realised I wouldn't have been the same player and anyway the maximum wage was still £20 a week.

I suppose Mr Johnston finally realised that my job really wasn't suitable for senior football when I had been rushed down to Bournemouth in a debonair wing commander's sports car, after playing 90 minutes for the station in the afternoon. I had arrived with five minutes to spare, dashing into the dressing room and onto the pitch. There was no wonder that I was a passenger that evening and there were no substitutes in those days. My Reading career was over, although, as the true gentleman he was, Harry Johnston assured me he realised how hard I had tried to cope with RAF life and football and he really appreciated what I had done for the club. What a wonderful gentleman. Another of my lifetime heroes!

I had been very proud to have been on their books as an amateur for seven years. The highlight for me had been playing for the Reserves against Birmingham City at St Andrews meeting Gil Merrick and scoring a special goal against Southampton.

The Services were full of professional footballers at the time but as National Service was coming to an end, there was more room for amateur players in their representative sides. Good timing again!

Reading as a Player 1961 - 1962

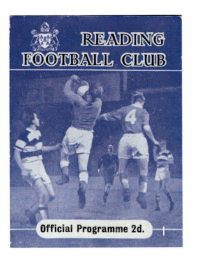

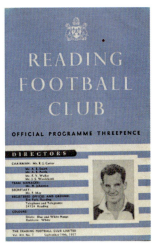

WILLIAMS SHOWS THE WAY

Reading Res. 2, Northampton Town Res. 2

TWO goals scored within a minute mid-way through the first half seemed to dim Reading Reserves hopes of winning their match with Northampton Town Reserves at Elm Park on Saturday, but credit must be given to the young Reading forward line for a grand fight back which salvaged a point (writes Bert May).

Newcomer Tony Williams, playing on the left-wing, started Reading's comeback with a fine goal direct from a corner—a feat which has not been performed at Elm Park since the days of Wilf Chitty.

The match opened at a rapid pace, with the Reading players serving up some grand football. They always looked like scoring and kept the "Cobblers" on the defensive for long stretches of the game. Gavan and Kirkup were always dangerous, and Williams shone on the wing until an injury slowed him up - although he continued to play well.

In defence, McLaren and Davies were sound, whilst wing-halves Andrews and Tune gave fine support to their forwards.

Despite an injury to Williams, who was off the field for two minutes, the Reserves continued to dominate the play until Northampton broke away to score. The goal came as a result of a defensive error by Tune, which enabled the centre-forward, Bright, to elude Davies and crash the ball past Meeson (25 minutes).

Reading were not given a chance to recover, and from the re-start, the visitors again raced into the attack. A neat pass from right-half, Peacock, found Bright in the penalty area, and he hooked the ball first time. Meeson made no effort to save what looked like a wide shot, and the ball entered the top of the net.

Reading fought back however and would have overwhelmed Northampton except for brilliant work by Pickering, who looked unbeatable until Williams scored his wonder goal from the third of three successive corners after 4 minutes.

Unfortunately, the game deteriorated in the second half and play became scrappy. Fouls were common, and the youthful home attack was caught in the off-side trap on numerous occasions.

Whilst in the first-half the crowd saw some fine flowing movements, in the latter half, attacks came from lone attempts by players trying to walk the ball the length of the pitch.

Penford, Tune, Andrews and Kirkup all tried shots, but the ball went wide every time. It began to look like Reading were to lose the game when Kirkup passed to Hood, and he lobbed the ball over the advancing 'keeper's head for the equalizer. The right-back kicked the ball out desperately but the referee allowed the goal.

Reading Reserves: Meeson; McLaren, Penford; Tune, Davies, Andrews; Beazley, Kirkup, Gavin, Hood, Williams.

Northampton Reserves: Pickering, Collins, Claypole; Peacock, Bre... Hall; Curtis, Miller, Bright, ... H. Haskins.

35

Opposite. Dougie Webb who scored over 100 goals for Reading

2. A very proud amateur was invited to join the official Reading FC squad for the season 1961 - 1962

1. Two treasured Reading programmes and I felt it was an honour to be included in the official pre-season Reading club photo

3. A very proud amateur was invited to join the official Reading FC squad photo for season 1961-192

Redhill 1961 - 1962

I started the 1962-1963 with 'K's' as Peter Gleeson, the Kingstonian manager had invited me to join them on a tour to Belgium out of season. I always seemed to have scored against K's with Casuals and Peter seemed happy to give me a game. Old friend Brian Wakefield was their regular goalkeeper with superb amateur players such as Hugh Lindsay, Rod Haider and Norman Field who would be brilliant to play alongside.

However, I learned the lesson that its never a good idea to join a club unless they have actually made you an offer. I joined and felt very guilty about leaving The Casuals and although I scored three in five games for K's, I couldn't get to training from Andover every week so I couldn't really challenge for a first team place. I hadn't been very sensible and I had behaved badly towards two clubs.

Frank Butterworth was manager of Redhill another Surrey club and I received an encouraging phone call from him in the officers mess late one evening, after having retired for the night. It must be important at midnight I thought - 'Good evening son, you need a club I need a striker- we're made for each other".

I was really impressed by his enthusiasm. Frank's approach was always direct and as an East Londoner, who had enjoyed a long playing career, he was superb to play for and the 'expenses' he offered added to Reading's contribution, meant I was earning more as a far from top level amateur player, than I was as an RAF Officer!

Incidentally, Mr May the long serving Reading Secretary had not been keen to give me any subsistence. 'You're an amateur- and amateurs don't get paid!

'But I do have honest expenses coming from Andover every time I play and I do need to eat if I am away a long time.' 'All right Williams, but I'll be watching out for your claims!' Luckily Harry Johnston and Bobby Campbell were a bit friendlier.

Redhill Football Club were very different. They played in The Athenian League and had a reputation throughout Non-League football for 'desperate defending' and whenever a player booted the ball out of the ground in any Non-League match, the call of 'Redhill' would be shouted by spectators especially in the South London grounds!

My first game for Frank was at Southall and I've never had so many attempts at goal with my head. The centres were driven across goal and I was really flying. It was one of those days when I kept connecting with 'Nat Lofthouse headers' but I hit the post twice, the keeper saved one with his face and a full back cleared one off the line. I thought it was my day but it wasn't! We lost 1-2 but at least the manager knew he'd signed someone who cared!

Frank Butterworth patched together a fine balance of skilful players, with experienced no nonsense defenders. He encouraged me to introduce some RAF and Old Malvernian colleagues and as a traditional East End Cockney he was surprisingly keen for me to play for my Old Boys in important cup matches, which even Casuals had been a bit worried about.

The ground was off the main road right in the middle of Redhill, with a small club room under the stand which was the scene for some excellent Saturday night parties and Frank steadily took Redhill up the table after a terrible start. I played up front with an amazing striker and wonderful character called Norman Dearlove, who was the epitome of someone who would 'run through brick walls for the team'.

It had been a great second half to the season which had earned me selection for Hampshire v Sussex, presumably qualifying because I was stationed at Andover.

The Athenian League was always respected for its social skills and the end of season dinner was an occasion not to be missed. The number of club members representing Redhill at the league dinner in the photo (3), indicated the club spirit that Frank Butterworth (leaning forward with hands on knees) had developed.

But Frank Butterworth's future wasn't certain at Redhill and Peter Gleeson had offered me a trip to Belgium on Kingstonian's Whitsun tour and I did reward him with four goals in two games including my only hat trick in senior football. The social side to the trip was memorable and I thought possibly my luck had changed and there was a future with Kingstonian after all.

I did start the 1962-63 season with Kingstonian but the traveling from Hereford and RAF duties once again prevented me from challenging seriously for a regular place and my last game for the special club included a goal in a 3-1 FA Cup win over local rivals Walton & Hersham. It was the second time I had left a club after playing the Surrey rivals but at least this time we had won!

Redhill 1961 - 1962

1. Giant keeper Fred Dakin intercepts a cross meant for Wimbeldon's Eddie Reynolds

2. Frank Butterworth a very popular manager from the East End of London

3. The spirit of Redhill is underlined by the massive turnout for Frank Butterworth at the Athenian League Annual Dinner.

4. Another great save from Fred Dakin this time to foil Wimbledon's fearsome striker Eddie Reynolds.

Redhill 1961 - 1962

1. David Loader a Malvernian friend with whom I played for seven clubs. Seen here for Redhill against Enfield.

3. During my limited appearances for the excellent Kingstonian club; beaten to the ball by St Albans City goalkeeper

2. David Loader v Southall

4. Norman Dearlove a great attacking partner at Redhill

5. Scoring an FA Cup goal against Walton & Hersham.

RAF Football 1962 - 63

Sky Blue Memories

By Flight Lieutenant AK Williams (former RAF Blue) and now editor and publisher of Football Directories

In 1958, I was one of the last recruits lucky enough to be called up for National Service. I say 'lucky' because today many youngsters leaving school find life particularly difficult as they struggle to come to terms with the ideals, standards and work opportunities of the huge adult world. We were given a very useful 'cushion' between school and the serious business of making a living and, as I had also been lucky enough to have passed a pre-selection course, I was sent straight to officer training at RAF Jurby on the Isle of Man.

As the youngest member of my squadron, surrounded by very experienced senior NCOs and intellectually superior university graduates I was (for the only time I can remember in my life), fitter than my companions! I was a big fish in a little pool, as far as football was concerned, having played for England under 18 Schools and Reading reserves. Indeed, my first lesson in the 'importance of football' was when waiting for my final interview at the pre-selection course at Uxbridge, with one eye on the clock as the Spurs v West Ham cup replay was due on the Wednesday afternoon TV slot.

As a 'W' I was last and when the officer looked at my record he remarked on my football interest. He apparently was an Arsenal fan and we discussed their victory recently over my team, Birmingham City, and then he mentioned the televised game which was about to be featured on television and took me off to the Officers' Mess to watch it. As far as I can remember we didn't talk about anything other than football and I finished top of the course. There was a lesson to be learnt there somewhere!

So it was off to Jurby an 'overseas' posting and possible qualification for a record on Sunday lunchtimes 'Forces Favourites'! The clerk of works at the RAF station was an official of Peel Football Club and I signed for them. The standard can't have been very good as I started with four hat tricks and finished with 24 in ten games. However we won the League and Cup 'double' and it was great fun. The fact that the RAF Jurby side beat the Island XI probably put things in perspective.

The football 'influence' on life appeared to rear its head again when, having been told that I was passing the course reasonably comfortably, I was then informed after the last exam that I had been recoursed and would spend another twelve months on the island. The fact that the Station team was due to play in the Group Inter-Station championships at Uxbridge in the weeks ahead, and that there was a local cup final to play was probably incidental! Anyway the Isle of Man in the summer was no hardship for a single young officer!

When I was eventually posted to Cardington I was given the rivetingly interesting job of giving recruits the 'oath of allegiance' but the Warrant Officer, Mr Dutton, was another football fanatic and one of the office lads, Joe Hurlock was a superb centre-half with Erith and Belvedere. So between us we ran the Station side.

As an 'amateur' I was also allowed to sign on for Bedford Town (Southern) and Corinthian Casuals (Isthmian) while remaining on Reading's books and playing for whoever I could get to in my time off. Very hectic but extremely enjoyable. The RAF still had separate amateur and professional representative sides so I rarely played with the 'pros' but I did play with George Curtis (Coventry City) Ron Atkinson (Oxford United) on occasions and saw quite a lot of Dougie Webb (Neil's father) who was a good friend from my Reading days.

I soon realised that I was actually enjoying Service life so the chart on which I had been brainwashed into ticking off the days to demob became a waste of time. I signed on for another spell and this time was lucky enough to go to Maintenance Command Headquarters, originally at Amport and then at Andover.

I suspect football had something to do with this as well as another soccer 'nut', Bill Cox in charge of personnel at Command, knew I was kicking my heels at RAF Hendon waiting for a posting and asked the AOC, who was doing his annual inspection, if he would like to interview me for his ADC's job.

What a glorious posting this turned out to be! The boss was Air Vice-Marshal Reilly, a lovely man who was keen on sport, had a daughter of twenty and was proud of the fact that I played football and cricket reasonably well! In one year at Andover I had over 200 days off for sport and, with a very lively social life, it was a blissful existence. Although I played for Reading reserves again at this time and achieved a personal ambition of playing at St Andrews, Birmingham, I also realised that perhaps my original dedication to the game was slipping.

Another 'duty' at this time was secretary of 'Icarus' (the RAF officers' team) and it was with this bunch of quite incredible characters that I 'grew up' and realised there was more to life than football! The Icarus tours will be memorable to say the least and we could also play a bit. In 1965, Icarus had five or six officers in the full RAF side and we could face the rest of the Air Force on equal terms. This was previously unheard of as officers in the Services were all supposed to be rugby types.

Among the Icarus players in those days were Ross Menzies (ex Glasgow Rangers and Cardiff City), Ralph Ramshaw (ex Sunderland), Chris Riley (ex Crewe Alexandra) and Keith Thomas (ex Sheffield Wednesday) with Roger Unwin, Tony Barret, Ginger Ayres and myself as full RAF Representative players and experienced amateur club players in Peter Cooper, Norman Jennings, Ray Greenhall, and Peter Graves. Sadly Ralph, Chris, and Tony have all since died in separate accidents but what a pleasure it was playing with them all and our two Argonaut Trophy successes will always give wonderful memories.

Since leaving the Royal Air Force a number of old Service friends have helped me out at the clubs where I have coached or managed. These clubs were usually better socially than they were on the field but they were always happy places to be! Ron Tinsley, my old striking partner in the RAF side (25 goals between us one season) played for Harrow Borough and Hungerford with his great mate, Micky Calvert, who also helped me at Epsom and Ewell. Indeed, the club to whom I owe most allegiance and still try to help, Hungerford Town, now possesses an RAF stalwart in David Dodds as joint manager and Roger Unwin has also managed the club.

When I was manager, John Lamb, a very successful past captain and coach of the RAF side, was my skipper and we also received excellent service from John Parkin, Norman Hudson and Ronnie Foster in the Seventies, while in recent seasons Alan Pluckrose, Graham Hearn, Mark Mallinson, Nicky Oswald, and Nick Truman have all been valued members of the club.

A common characteristic of all these lads was the ability to work hard at their football and 'play' hard socially. Their general attitude and bearing was outstanding and they gave the club an extra dimension. I certainly learnt a lot from my time in the Royal Air Force; I still value the friendships I made and from what I can gather the spirit and fun of being a sportsman in the Service is still the same today.

Action from an Argonaut Trophy Final at Highbury. Icarus are on the attack and their centre forward obviously getting nowhere near this centre.

32 Goalmouth

'Sky Blue Memories' as published in the official RAF magazine

Royal Airforce Football Association Season 1963 - 64
RAF v FA Amateur XI
Back Row: Fg Off Williams, SAC N Taylor, Cpl AR White, LAC T Holmes, JnrTech RJ Jones, LAC HN Bevan, SAC D Jones, SAC E Weaver, Flt Sgt JT Connolly (trainer)
Seated: SAC Casagranda D, Sqn Ldr A White (Hon. Sec) , Flt Lt R Menzies (Capt), Gp Capt CM Fell (Chairman),
SAC GG Richardson.

RAF Football 1962 - 63

Although I had thoroughly enjoyed my coaching at Hallfield, I wasn't qualified to teach and apart from the football I really didn't fancy the life - although the holidays were impressive!

I had enjoyed the junior officers responsibilities in The Royal Air Force, but had joined in the national serviceman's game of counting down the days to my demob. Of course I had no experience of any other way of living and having looked around and discussed jobs with football colleagues, an RAF officer's life really seemed attractive, especially if I could carry on as an active sportsman at a reasonable standard.

Having played for the RAF amateur eleven during my national service, I was welcomed back enthusiastically and I reported to RAF Hendon, where administration was sorted out for the re-signing of returning servicemen until their postings were arranged.

We had the fun of playing on behalf of RAF Hendon in an RAF London Leagues Cup FInal at Uxbridge with a few 'guests' from Icarus and during my short stay in North London, the station had its annual inspection from the Air Officer Administration from Maintenance Command Headquarters at Amport near Andover.

Flight Lieutenant Bill Cox, who was organising the day for him, also apparently ran the football and cricket at Command. So when he heard I was waiting for a suitable posting, was on Reading's books and had played football for the RAF, he quickly suggested I should be interviewed by Air Vice Marshall Reilly while he was at Hendon. Then, if he thought I was suitable, perhaps I could fill the position of ADC for him back at Andover.

So once again the magic football wand was waved and I was given an extremely pleasant job of being personal assistant to the Air Vice Marshall, arranging all the inspections of the RAF stations in Maintenance Command.

I also took on the job of Secretary to Icarus FC, the RAF Officers Football team. Air Vice Marshall Reilly encouraged my involvement in all sports, including Maintenance Command HQ's cricket team which meant he was understanding about my days away from the office.

On one occasion when asking for permission to leave early on a Friday, to catch trains and boat to The Isle of Man where Icarus had a match, I was told very firmly 'No you can't you're in the RAF and I'm sure we can arrange a Maintenance aircraft to visit RAF Jurby on a duty run'! Not only did I get a flight to Jurby but it also took two other players and we all got a trip back after the week-end. What a wonderful boss!

The headquarters of Maintenance Command was moved from the village of Amport to the edge of the town of Andover. This meant moving from a delightful officers mess in a stately home to modern accommodation and the brand new office block. Before leaving we had to run down and close the bar in the officers mess and as there were only half a dozen officers living in, it was decided we would have an auction for the drinks but we would each take it turns to claim a bottle.

This sounded a great idea, but as we settled down I realised it was my turn (as the junior officer there) to claim every sixth bottle for a basic payment of £1. But there was no choice, I was just given whichever bottle the senior officers had decided was next! I finished up with a Green Chartreuse, Sweet Sherry and a selection of Beers! Certainly better than nothing! So I took them all home where the Green Chartreuse lasted two years!

Air Vice Marshall Reilly had invited me to dinner on a number of occasions where I met his very attractive daughter, but he was about to retire and the next boss wasn't so keen on sport.

Cricket was taken very seriously at Maintenance Command Headquarter where Two Flight Lieutenants, Leonard and Slade virtually carried the side through to win the Command inter station cup.

Being stationed at Andover and having failed my driving test a second time meant attending training in London was awkward. After starting the 1961-62 season with Corinthian Casuals I realised things just weren't the same and probably, having proved I could score goals at senior amateur level, I may have considered it was the right time to boost my limited income by playing for a club that paid 'expenses.' I was also still on Reading's books and had enjoyed my best run in the Reserves early in the season.

A secretarial refresher course was probably necessary after my comparative holiday at Maintenance Command and I reported to RAF Spitalgate near Grantham in Lincolnshire. Once again Mr Johnston, my wonderful manager at Reading, notified Grantham Town football club, giving permission for me to train with them.

RAF Course Grantham

I fully realised while on this course, that I really didn't want to be working in secretarial admin for the rest of my career. This was so different from the RAF sport and social life I had experienced so far.

Obviously this was a very irresponsible attitude, but I was pleased to be invited to play for Grantham Town away to Spalding United in the Midland League and although we won 4-1, I strained a hamstring for the first and only time of my life and didn't play for another five weeks.

I met an old friend whose family ran a hotel in the town and on one occasion when driving back to the station, gave a lift to one of the WRAF girls waiting at a bus stop. Apparently her job was printing the end of course admin test papers that we would soon be taking!

RAF Football 1962 - 63

1. Officers Mess at RAF Amport, the original Maintenance Command Headquarters

3. Another AOC's inspection with the new boss

5. Dancing with Penny Crauford at Halton Summer Ball

2. My first AOC's inspections for Maintenance Command

4. The secretarial course at RAF Grantham

6. The RAF Hereford Ball with guests, Margaret, Denis & Eileen Saunders and Corinthian-Casuals secretary Bill Whickson and his wife.

RAF Football 1962 - 63

RAF Hereford and Hereford United 1963-1964

I only just scraped through this exam and I travelled to Hereford, as the new Adjutant for Group Captain Edmonds at the Boy Entrants Wing at RAF Hereford after the Christmas holidays. When I reported in I was welcomed with a bollocking from my new boss - he knew I should have done better on the course!

Severe winter weather had virtually closed down roads across the country since Christmas, but once again Harry Johnston had been in touch with the local club on my behalf. On this occasion it was Ray Daniel at Hereford United who allowed me to train at Edgar Street and possibly be given a few games, for which he very generously offered me £6 per match.

This was all very well, but by mid February the icy spell was still dominating the country and no football had been played. I had settled down as assistant to Group Captain Edmonds, my best ever boss, who was a true caricature of the traditional RAF pilot as we had been brought up to recognise in war films. He had been honoured as a brave pilot and his social skills matched those we had seen on the screen, but he was also a stickler for hard work and the correct way of conducting oneself. In fact he was probably the father figure I had missed since Dad's death and what's more he had two charming daughters!

Hereford had a thriving jazz club, to which all the best traditional jazz bands visited and there seemed to be a regular meeting for the local nurses to meet the RAF lads, but junior officers had to be careful!

I had to wait until Saturday 9th March before Hereford Reserves had a match in which I was invited to play, and we beat Stafford Rangers Reserves 7-0. I managed a couple but the star of the Reserve team was another Williams. Roy had scored over 200 goals for the club and the second team was now benefitting from his experience. Games came thick and fast as the club had to catch up with all the fixtures affected by the cold spell. Consequently we were playing three games a week and Mr Daniel was as good as his word, which meant I received £18 a week - once again more than my RAF pay!

Playing alongside me in the Station side at Hereford was Bob Reeves, a brilliant goalscorer, who really should have been a full RAF representative player but somehow had been overlooked. It was great playing with Bob and he also invited me to join his civilian club Belmont Rangers, with whom we won The Herefordshire County Senior Cup at the end of the season.

Of course Hereford was just over the Malvern Hills from the school and it was good to see Denis and Eileen Saunders quite regularly. The 1962-1963 season had been extended because of the terrible winter so there was little time before the next season's training started. I had enjoyed a weeks coaching course and was feeling reasonably fit so decided to make an effort and travel to London and rejoin The Corinthian-Casuals if they would have me. It would also be fun to spend week-ends in London.

RAF Halton & Wycombe Wanderers 1964

My last posting in The Royal Air Force was RAF Halton near Aylesbury in Technical Training Command. The Officers Mess was in a glorious stately home with magnificent grounds. My job was similar to Hereford, as an adjutant for an Apprentice Wing and my boss was a pilot who insisted in taking me up for flights in very small training aircraft, which I must say worried me a little.

An Icarus colleague apparently had recommended me to Wycombe Wanderers, as I was now stationed nearby. I really wasn't happy with the idea of joining one of the best amateur clubs, as I knew I had been disappointing with Corinthian-Casuals and Kingstonian.

Perhaps playing with better players would be easier. Well, very soon after signing and having filled in on the left wing for the first team in a victory at Hendon, I returned to the reserves and must say found it very strange playing at Loakes Park with a severe slope from one wing to another. Manager at the time was Don Welsh, a very original character, who had captained Charlton in their FA Cup final success in 1947 and it had been an honour to wear such a famous club's colours.

However, I had decided once and for all, that I really wasn't dedicated to the RAF and my mother would certainly appreciate some help, as she was planning to open up a bed and breakfast in Guernsey. Life in the Channel Islands presented an exciting prospect, I was, after all, still single and free to go wherever I liked. while St Martins seemed a super football club!

I kept in contact with Icarus and was invited to play occasionally, as retired RAF Officers could remain playing members of the Club. In fact, after two years in The Channel Islands I had the pleasure of playing with a very strong Icarus side that beat the full Royal Air Force team by 4-3 - a very satisfying and unexpected result !

RAF Football 1962 - 63

1. Tech Training Command who beat REME 5-2

2. RAF Hereford celebrate with skipper Reeves

3. RAF Ball at Halton. The two lads helping were team mates in the station football team and my guests with their ladies were Brian Wakefield and Martin Black from Corinthian Casuals.

4. Maintenancem HQ Cricket team

5. Cricket at Andover: Opening the Batting with Squadron Leader Partridge

RAF Football 1962 - 63

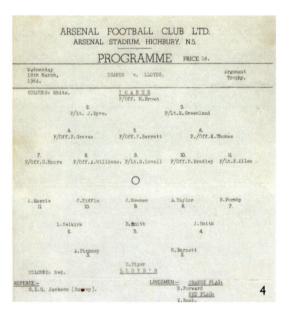

1. The Cup Final at Highbury: The skipper
2. Icarus FC
3. Football at Hereford: A goal for Hereford Reserves
4. Belmont Rangers who won The Herefordshire Senior Cup
   Back row, left to right: Handley, Newman, Hill, Munn, Rich and Braithwaite (Captain)
   Front Row: Bennett, T. Buchanan, Williams, Reeves and B. Buchanan
5. The Cup Final team sheets

Sir Stanley Rous's Plans

Sir Stanley Rous was the senior Executive at the Football Association, who were responsible for all levels of the game in this country, while the Cup Finals of The FA Challenge Cup and The FA Amateur Cup were the respective highlights of the English professional and amateur football seasons.

Sir Stanley was well respected as a real football man who actually cared about the game at all levels and the country itself. He included a message in The Football Association's official FA Yearbook and looking back at that decade it's interesting to note some of the issues that were presented by the senior official.

He was convinced our national winter sport should be for 'the common man' i.e. the man on the terrace or on the park touchline; their views should be heard. The genuine character of the British public's love for the game would always support football, but we should listen to their views. With more and more football being televised, the game's attraction would be enjoyed by millions but we should be careful not to become too serious about soccer. It is a game which still exists for people's enjoyment.

Referees should also receive guidance on their general attitude. Public Institutions, (such as The Football Association) could quite naturally become set in their ways, they were apt to become too timorous of new ideas and cling to outmoded practices. For example, it was important that the development of floodlighting at matches and introducing more youth coaching and competitions for the young, should be considered important throughout the country.

Midway through the 'fifties' Sir Stanley's worries included:-
a) Should there be less League games in a Season?

b) Should overseas clubs be invited to play more pre-season friendlies in England to help our general football education?

c) Examples of bad temper, lack of sportsmanship and flouting the referees decisions reflect badly on the individual, the game the club, the league and the country. Winning is important, but not if it means losing self respect or public support.

d) Should there be a National Youth League?
The lifting of Entertainment Tax is welcomed, but more money must be made available for the game to improve facilities and better coaching for the young throughout the country.

As the Fifties were coming to an end Sir Stanley Rous had more warnings for us all:

a) More Games instructors to be made available at public parks with more free-lance coaches encouraged to help all sports at all purpose recreation centres, plus better social facilities at sports grounds of all sizes

b) Much more must be done to attract the youth of the country into football clubs to train, play and watch.

c) More coaches and more playing fields must be found.

d) Air travel and television makes international football more popular for all ages.

e) Sunday football should be recognized.

f) Has a Ministry of Sport been considered ?

Is it different today?

This article, by F.A. Senior Executive Sir Stanley Rouse, was written regarding his views on Association Football in the early ' nineteen fifties'. He really cared for the game and often wore his heart on his sleeve, but at least he could be seen to be helping all levels of the game during his time in charge of the country's football.

Who is seen to care about the image of the game and its future in the modern football world ?

Old Malvernians 1958 -1969

The Old Malvernian Football Club has enjoyed a distinguished history since its formation in 1897, as can be seen from the feature on page 47. Football at Malvern College flourished when cared for by masters who loved the game like Harvey Chadder and Denis Saunders, but sadly, executives running the modern school have decided to play Rugby Union in the Autumn term and Association Football in the Spring term. Consequently the standard of the school's winter sports are now both second rate. As they cannot compete with fixtures against their traditional school rivals who play in the Christmas term.

I was really lucky to have arrived at the school as Denis Saunders took over the football coaching at Malvern. He had captained the famous Pegasus Football Club for Oxford and Cambridge University graduates in every competitive game that the comparatively new club had played. This of course included two Wembley victories when Pegasus had won the FA Amateur Cup in front of 100,000 attendance in 1951 and 1953.

Pegasus had been coached along the push and run style successfully adopted by Tottenham Hotspur, so with Denis Saunders coaching the Malvern first eleven, a constant flow of well drilled footballers passed through the school. Many continued to enjoy playing the same style with the school Old Boys in the famous Arthur Dunn Cup and the relatively new Arthurian League, which had been developed in the home counties.

I had enjoyed three years of top class coaching in which Denis Saunders' teams were unbeaten in inter school matches. I had been whisked off to the RAF for national service so didn't have a natural link with the weekly old boys fixtures, but can remember being excited when, later in the season, I was asked to play in an Authur Dunn cup tie away at Shrewsbury School against the Old Salopians in the 1958-1959 season.

I obviously had played with some of the younger lads at school and against the older ones in the annual Old Boys match, but this was in the famous competition against a school I knew well from the last three years fixtures. We had never lost to Shrewsbury and I was fit from Reading coaching and RAF life and had never felt better.

What's more we were taking it seriously, staying away in a hotel on the Friday night and discussing the game and suggested tactics like a senior club. I was impressed with the attitude of the older players and Denis Saunders' influence had certainly rubbed off on all the younger ones.

We won the game 5-3 and much to my disappointment I didn't score and we eventually lost in the semi-final to Old Cholmleans, from Highgate School, who had enjoyed a great spell of school success before Malvern's push and run era.

However, my best memory of playing at Shrewsbury occured the next year when we were drawn away again and this time I managed a hat trick. This including a goal starting on the right wing and a run in which I produced the Ronnie Allen foot over the ball trick three times successfully, including a dummy sold to the goalkeeper. I was severely ticked off for unbecoming behaviour as my celebrations were considered out of order!

However we reached the final and met old rivals Old Reptonians at Wealdstone. David Loader had sent over a perfect centre and I was able to score with a 'Nat Lofthouse' header at the far post to equalise with ten minutes to go. I remember my attitude was frowned upon when I screamed at mid field star Mike Theobald to go down as his injury prevented him running. The brave Mike stumbled on and his inside forward Citroen scored the winner for Repton. In to-days football, players go down without being touched, quite the opposite to the bravery Mike showed, but all the same he needed treatment and we might have at least shared the trophy.

Celebrations after successful Arthur Dunn ties were the best. We had some superb social stars and we always made sure we stayed the night together after cup ties. Sadly, many of the best Malvernian players weren't always available but the two outstanding inspirational match winners Ian Ryder-Smith and Jan Bridle usually were!

Ian Ryder-Smith outgrew his strength at school and left as a gawky 6ft 4inch middle league player. However he became an outstanding member of the The Old Malvernian Football Club. He enjoyed the social side immensely, but found that as he filled out, he realised he had excellent stamina and became an inspirational mid field dynamo who was huge and could tackle, jump his full height and score goals including penalties. He was the perfect leader and as he was usually surrounded by truly talented players with all the different skills, Ian was in a perfect situation.

Another outstanding star was Jan Bridle, christened Jan Illaszewicz, son of a Polish wartime fighter pilot. Jan was not very tall or very fast but he could control a ball from any angle under any pressure and would get his shots away with hardly any back lift. His eye for goal was second to none and he was easily the best goalscorer in the history of the school and the Old Malvernians. His statistics of Arthur Dunn goals and seven Dunn successes out of twelve finals are competition records that one cannot imagine ever being overtaken.

David Loader remained a great friend all of his life which tragically ended from cancer far too early. We played together for Malvern, a Newbury Sunday side, Corinthian-Casuals, Reading 'A', Old Malvernians, Donnington Village and Redhill. He was a very skillful speedy right winger who scored plenty of goals and was also an excellent clarinet player who played in a good standard of jazzband. His sister Helen was a keen supporter and as our families lived near Newbury, we enjoyed many musical evenings together.

Old Malvernians 1958 - 1969

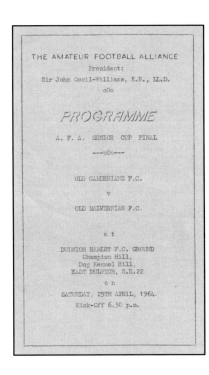

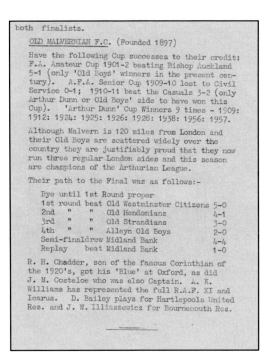

1. 1959-1960
Runners Up in my first final. Old Reptonians win 3-2.
Back row: Mike Theobald, Johnnie Woods, Peter Jagger, David Martin, Tony Williams and David Loader,
Front row: Mike Costeloe, David Brough, Tony Beeson, Richard Chadder and Ian MacLaurin

2. 1966-1967
Losing finalists. Old Brentwoods win 3-2
Back row: Peter Townend, Jan Bridle, David Bailey, Tony Williams, Roger Tolchard and Phil Hayden
Front Row: David Loader Bill Stevens, Ian Ryder-Smith, Richard Chadder and Tony Beeson.

Old Malvernians 1958 - 1969

Another lifetime friend, Bill Stevens holds me responsible (gratefully I hope) for his long and happy marriage to Jackie. Our Arthur Dunn Cup matches at home would be played at Malvern, often in front of substantial schoolboy support and afterwards we would entertain the visitors and then enjoy a party at one of the local hotels. On this occasion I had suggested to the school secretaries in the admin office that they should come along and join us, hopefully with some celebrations after the cup tie. Jackie did come, met Bill and they have been together ever since, buying a lovely house in West London which probably makes them millionaires to-day.

I enjoyed many sleep overs with Bill and Jackie in London and we always remembered Bill's winning goal in the AFA Cup Semi-Final against The Civil Service. He usually played on the left wing, where his strength and heading ability often provided vital goals. So we had power on the left and speedy skills from David Loader on the right.

Probably the best pound for pound player was David Marnham a strong dominating centre half with good control and passing ability. But he was hardly ever available, having worked abroad a great deal. Our West Bromwich Albion coaches saw him play just once and wanted to sign him on the spot.

My Arthur Dunn Cup contributions came to an end after 14 seasons in which the club had competed in 50 ties of which I had been involved in 40. I was normally playing for my Saturday club on most week-ends but over the years I had played for the OMs in 121 games, playing in every position accept right wing, and scored 107 goals. It was a privilege and always great fun playing in the Denis Saunders way and relaxing afterwards as one did in those days!!

The friends I have made through Malvern football and indeed with our rivals such as Repton and Brentwood, will be treasured for the rest of my life and I will always appreciate the initiative shown by my Prep School headmaster Mr Rigby to get me that interview for a football scholarship at Malvern.

1. 1968-1969
   Winners against Old Bradfieldsians 1-0
   Back row : Roger Tolchard, Peter Townend, Tim Begg, Michael Walker-Smith, Rob Erhardt, Mike Driver,
   Front row: Phil Hayden, David Loader, Ian Ryder-Smith, Tony Williams and Jan Bridle.

2. One coudn't wish for more!
   A headed goal in a cup final against our fiercest rivals, The Old Reptonians

Old Malvernians - 100 Years Young

Old Malvernians - 100 Years Young

An Appreciation of Malvernian Football by Tony Williams as The Old Malvernian F.C. celebrates its Centenary

"Work hard for your exams and you are on your way to Solihull Grammar School - a rugby playing school." That was the message in my last year at Edgbaston Prep School, but suddenly overnight I was on my way to Malvern for an interview with the headmaster and I had been offered a 'Football Scholarship' and a place at Malvern College.

I now had a reason to work and passed the 'Common Entrance Exam' with 'A' grades in everything - I really wanted to play with a round ball! At Malvern I was going to a school with a football tradition. Malvernian Full English Internationals included:
A. H. Stratford - T. M. Pilse - F. W. Hargreaves - J. Hargreaves - D. H. Greenwood - C. J. Burnup - R. E. Foster - R. Corbett - S. H. Day
Amateur Internationals: C. C. Page - G. B. Cannery - J. W. Stretton - A P. Day - G. N. Foster - G. B. Partridge - W. H. L. Lister

The Old Malvernians had won the Amateur Cup by beating Bishop Auckland 5-1 in 1902 when the team was:
C. Tuff, C. H. Ransome, G. H. Simpson-Hayward, A. N. Todd, G. B. Cannery, E. H. Simpson, S. H. Day, B. S. Foster, P. N. Sutherland-Graeme, R. E. Foster and R. Corbett.

However, by the time I arrived in 1952, school results had not been good, in fact sport hadn't been taken very seriously at all.

Nevertheless, Pegasus, that wonderful club made up of Oxford and Cambridge 'Blues' who didn't even play in a league, had just won the FA Amateur Cup twice (beating Harwich & Parkeston and Bishop Auckland in front of 100,000 crowds) and their captain, a convert of Arthur Rowe and Vic Buckingham's push and run system (the same sort of style that Liverpool played in the eighties) was to be signed on as a geography master at Malvern College.

Denis Saunders, for it was he, changed the whole thinking of the school as far as football was concerned.

The first eleven was undefeated for five years and in three consecutive years two players from the College were selected for England Under 18's They were David Marnham and Mike Costello

1955, Paul Walton and David French 1956 and Mike Theobald (captain) and myself 1957.

Many of us played with professional clubs. At Reading with me were David Loader and Chris Styles and when we were linked with the club in the Sunday Express, a Malvern housemaster seriously suggested we sued the paper for linking public schoolboys with professional football! The Malvern team only lost 1-2 to the full Pegasus side and 1-3 to the W.B.A. Youth team and were the first winners of the Schools Six-a-Sides, held at Brentwood in 1957.

We loved our football and played in every spare moment. As we left the school (and I cried myself to sleep in my last term as I enjoyed it so much) we joined the Old Malvernians and as we all played a

> "Work hard for your exams and you are on your way to Solihull Grammar School - a rugby playing school."

'push and run' system it was easy to fit in.

Many of us played with senior non-league clubs but we all turned up for the Arthur Dunn Cup. In 23 years (between 1956 and 1978) we won the cup nine times from fifteen finals, and reached an A.F.A. Senior Final. The comradeship, pride and respect for each other and the man who made it happen (Denis Saunders) was probably one of the most wonderful parts of my life.

The friends and team mates from those days are still valued today, and some of them haven't done badly! Lord MacLaurin President of E & W TCCB (ex O.M's and Tescos), Bryan Richardson, the Coventry City chairman and Peter Ellis, a brilliant goalscorer who is on the board of QPR and is an ex-chairman, are sportsmen who are influencing modern sport in the best possible way.

Footballers amongst the public schools old boys in the early Sixties could have produced another 'Pegasus' and although some of us tried to bond together with Corinthian Casuals, the lure of money was too much as we no longer came from privileged families. We needed the cash and sadly we split up to play for other clubs.

Playing for Malvern College in an unbeaten school side for three years and then having the privilege of learning about Arthur Dunn football

from the likes of Richard Chadder, Tony Beeson and David Marnham was great. Then as mature players we had a superb captain in Ian Ryder-Smith, and possibly the best goalscorer, to be capped in the old amateur international days in Jan Bridle. He once scored twice when an A.F.A. XI drew 2-2 with the full England Amateur International XI (disguised as an F.A. XI) and regularly played for Bournemouth Reserves. He holds the record for Arthur Dunn goals and appearances and played in a record seven winning Dunn sides out of twelve finals! He was a superb player.

The Old Malvernians of that era had class, determination and spirit. Anyone in football lucky enough to experience this type of club will remember it for the rest of their lives.

I'm someone whose whole life has been dominated by football. I enjoyed the luck of being taught the game by Denis Saunders and the privilege of playing with some truly special Arthurian players. At this level, could I ask for more? If there is another school producing a similar dynasty then good luck to them; they will have something to lovingly remember all their lives.

The best ten Malvernian players I played with in a modern 3-5-2 formation were probably:-

Paul Walton

Ian Ryder-Smith - David Marnham - Ian Preston Jones

David Loader - Mike Theobald - David French

Ian MacLaurin - Bill Stevens

Tony Williams - Jan Bridle

The Old Malvernians Football Club is now 100 years old. We have produced Full Internationals, Amateur Internationals and Schoolboy Internationals. Our Arthur Dunn record is very reasonable and as a Midland school playing in London in the Arthurian League we have held our own until recently as the influx of girls to the school gives us less six formers to pick from for school elevens and our supply of 'talent' has decreased from the football viewpoint!

Maybe there won't be many more football fanatics like me emerging from Malvern College (that's probably a good thing for the school), but at least I can say a big thank you for all the satisfaction and pleasure I received from being part of a very, special football era at a very special school.

60-70 OMFC - AFA

Richard Chadder celebrates with the Cup and the happy squad, having beaten Old Reptonians 2-1 are,
from left to right:
David Loader, David Bailey (crouching), Tony Williams, Mike Costeloe (hidden), David Marnham, Ian Ryder-Smith, Tony Beeson, Bill Stevens and Tony Theobald plus Jan Illaszewicz missing.

Channel Islands 1964 - 65

Mum in Guernsey

Early in the Sixties my mother had moved to Guernsey in The Channel Islands to look after her brother who had no family and whose wife had died. The idea of starting a 'Bed and Breakfast' business with her appealed, so I left the Air Force after five very happy years.

Guernsey was a wonderful place for a single 25 year old sportsman to be living and I was lucky to be invited to sign for St Martins Football Club who had a brilliant young football squad. They were an absolute pleasure to play with for the 1964-1965 season.

I was engaged to a lovely Essex girl Penny Crauford, but it was difficult to build on the relationship, as I was in the Channel Islands and we both eventually agreed there was no future for us together.'

Our skipper at the club was Colin Renouf, who I think could have been as good as the famous Welsh International giant John Charles. He had the physical power to dominate at centre half or centre forward and his heading power was as good as anyone I have seen (other than Nat Lofthouse) -but I don't think Nat could have played as well at centre half!. However, Colin didn't want to leave the Island as a youngster and turned down a multitude of offers from League Clubs.

Joining the Guernsey champions and playing against one of the least powerful clubs in my first league match, should have been an easy settling in period. I did manage a goal but we lost badly and Saints supporters must have wondered what had happened to their outstanding team. We had already beaten Sylvans 8-4 and 5-2 in pre season friendlies.

The season settled down and it was great fun playing in such a good side. Gerve Brazier was the excellent Island goalkeeper and mid field was usually dominated by Jack Martel and Barry Toulier. The back four including John Forsey, the club's classy centre half and a very promising and versatile defender John Herpe were not often tested.

In most fixtures Saints were usually on the attack as the power of Colin Renouf and speed of John Loveridge was prompted by the scheming of 'Dooney' Russell. I was given the No 11 shirt, as their previous left winger had joined a rival club, but coach Jack Loveridge knew I was a central striker and gave me the freedom to roam wherever I liked.

The system worked very well and we won twenty of the next twenty one games - the other was drawn! Our first defeat was a thrilling 4-5 battle against Belgraves, who were inspired by my good friend Bonny Eldridge, who scored twice and also dominated in mid field.

St Martins proved to be too strong, although Belgraves had spoiled their unbeaten run and we did lose an inter Island cup tie against Jersey's Oaklands FC. The mid season arrival of right winger Arthur Pugh, a speedy ex Non-League player from Northern England really took Saints into a different level and the Priaux League Championship was won with just one defeat and over 100 goals.

The Island team had regular representative games during the season so that by the end of the campaign a regular squad should be in place. Matt Le Tissier's father Marcus played in some of the games and all his family have contributed greatly to the development of Guernsey football in recent years.

The Champions of Guernsey traditionally play their Jersey counterparts for The Upton Trophy at the end of every season. It was Jersey's turn to host this season's Champions decider and Georgetown FC were representing Jersey.

The Referee was the experienced Jim Finney, an old friend from my RAF Hereford days and one of the best officials in the game. We had a quiet first half but a final 3-1 scoreline brought Saints the Upton Trophy for the second consecutive year and provided one of my very best days in the game.

To play for Guernsey against Jersey for the 'Muratti Vase' is a special privilege and one I enjoyed (especially the goal), apart from a lunatic section of the crowd stopping the game when we were 2-1 up and the coach's insistence that we should play to his system rather than the players strengths.

The team was selected by a committee made up of members of the league clubs. Sometimes the senior clubs, even if they had not enjoyed a good season, would have a player selected so they would be represented in the Muratti. This policy didn't help.

We also had an FA Coach brought in from England to prepare the side for the big game. However, he obviously didn't know the players strengths or why they had been picked. I felt particularly angry about this, as I had been selected as the No11, but as my season with St Martins had proved, I was a roving striker alongside Colin Renouf and John Loveridge and not a left winger. After all we had scored over 20 goals each in a very successful campaign.

Channel Islands 1964 - 65

1. It was a privilege to play with this St Martins squad.
   Players back row, left to right: Marshall, Forsey, Brazier, Martell, Tullier, Herpe and Gorvel
   Front Row: Pugh, Loveridge, Renouf, Russell and Williams.

2. Engaged to Penny Crauford

3. Muratti Vase Programme

4. First Saints goal but defeated 1-3 by Sylvans

5. My favourite picture of Colin Renouf - the height, the balance and the power!

6. A headed goal for St. Martins but without the Renouf style

7. A goal against The Northerners at St Martins

Channel Islands 1964 - 65

For the Muratti, I was told by the coach that as a left winger I should hug the line and stretch the opposition, but I hardly touched the ball and only scored my goal by sneaking into the box on one occasion.

We led 2-1 but after the crowd trouble, we never dominated the game again and the potential of a very good side was never really allowed to emerge. We lost and I was furious at the end of the game and took myself off to an obscure hotel restaurant to drown my sorrows. Not very sporting!

The family idea for a bed and breakfast wasn't turning out to be practical, although a lot of friends did come to stay at my Mother's house. So I scraped a living selling insurance and then helping to run a coffee bar with very little dedication.

Some of my friends I socialised with on the island were English football lads from the mainland, and we decided to join the bottom club Vale Recreation and play together in the following season. St Martins were without doubt going to win everything unless a challenge came from somewhere and we did help to provide just that.

I shared a flat with 'Bonnie 'Eldridge, a very good footballer who had played for Grays Athletic. He joined with his brother Dave and Noel Jefferies, a Guernsey lad and a very competitive mid field player, who had kicked me a few times in the previous season.

Also joining were ball playing inside forward Pete Mellor from Rangers, full backs Alan Hamon and Bob Bannister plus speedy left winger Kenny Giles from Northerners. The club already had a promising young goalkeeper Mick Falla, the experienced George Pearson and tough defenders Les Fallaize and Bruce Wallace.

This news really shook the football world on the Island and I must say we were not very popular with anyone accept the Vale Recreation committee, led by Jurat W.J.Corbet after whom the very smart enclosed ground with floodlights had been named 'The Corbet Field'. We introduced training twice a week, bought new kit and organised a regular match day programme to be regularly giving the supporters all the club news.

The local Sports Editor Rex Bennett had a field day and thoroughly enjoyed the regular news stories. 'Who do they think they are?' shouted many of the locals who labelled us outsiders even though half of Vale's new players were also Guernsey lads.

Being a small island, we might bump into aggressive football fans at any time, but our challenge to St Martins had the best possible effect on the local game, where attendances shot up and the press enjoyed an eventful season.

In another wonderful season of football, Vale Recreation won some silverware but St Martins beat us in a play off and I must say by the end of the season I was exhausted from the pressure, some high living and a lot of football I shouldn't have played with a few injuries. We had attracted crowds of over 1,000 to local Island league games and feelings were intense throughout the island, but it was fun and I think the Island football people look back with amazement at the interest that was created.

I had made a lot of special friends but I returned to the mainland for season 1966-1967 with Noel Jefferies who wanted to sample English Non-League football. We trained with Tooting & Mitcham United where my old Corinthian Casuals Coach Doug Flack was in charge. Noel enjoyed an excellent spell with the club and was also picked for Surrey, but having enjoyed my coaching in Guernsey I applied for, and was offered, the managers job at Athenian League Division Two club Epsom & Ewell.

Bonny Eldridge played for Guernsey again at the end of the 1965-1966 season and was a hero in Guernsey's Muratti victory over the old enemy. He was a wonderful player to have on your side, he never stopped running (he regularly appears in the goal mouth action photos looking for the half chance!)

Two tremendous years in the Channel Islands were packed with sporting ups and downs, a social whirlwind and a lot of memories that I will look back on with pleasure all my life. I even had the honour of representing the island in its traditional Rugby challenge match against Jersey for The Siam Cup which we won with a penalty kick, when the referee adjudged the kick to have gone over the top of an upright, to win the game for Guernsey in the last minute.

A suggestion that I might be able to promote Guernsey sport in England was discussed but since leaving the island I have returned to see friends regularly and also organised football tours for Jimmy Hills Football Weekly, Hungerford Town, Rothmans Representative Squad, Old Malvernians and North Curry Football Club and have followed the efforts of clubs from Jersey and Guernsey in the FA Vase over the years. During my time with Rothmans I was able to arrange sponsorship to the Channel Island leagues and we held the Rothmans Cup Semi-Finals and Finals in the Channel Islands.

In season 2011-2012 Guernsey FC entered a team in The Combined Counties DIvision One and won the championship scoring 138 goals. They moved up to The Premier Division and finished as runners-up after reaching the Semi-Final in The FA Vase. Their great season was capped by promotion to The Isthmian League Division One South where they contested the play offs in the 2013-2014 campaign.

The quite wonderful progress of Guernsey FC has been one of the best modern football stories and the support the club has received from the Island has been magnificent. I am very proud to have worn their green and white!

Channel Islands 1964 - 65

1. A 'Nat' header for Guernsey against Salisbury

3. A Muratti goal against Jersey watched by Bonny Eldridge

5. Guernsey 1965-66 (won 3-1 with goalscorer Bonny Eldridge one of the stars) *Back row left to right:* Allan Hamon, Micky Duncan, Richard Harvey, 'Gerve' Brazier, Colin Renoulf and John Herpe *Front row:* Arthur Pugh, John Loveridge, Bonny Eldridge, Ken Giles and Wally Torode.

2. Pre match hand shakes before the Guernsey Champions play the Jersey Champions for the Upton Park Trophy

4. Inter Island games always attracted a passionate crowd

6. Guernsey 1964 -65 (lost 1-2) *Back row left to right:* John Herpe, Noel Jeffries, 'Gerve' Brazier, Bob Brehaut, Roger Hemery and Lloyd Duquemin. *Front row:* Arthur Pugh, Colin Renoulf, Bonny Eldridge, John Loveridge and Tony Williams.

Channel Islands 1964 - 65

1. The winning Guernsey Rugby squad who beat Jersey with a last minute penalty kick in 1965

3 & 7. Vale Recreation's first team squad in Yellow and (in 3) the end of season trophies on display with all Vale's personnel

4. A Muratti goal for Bonny Eldridge helping Guernsey to a 3-1 victory in 1966

2 & 5. Proud skipper of Vale Recreation

6. A header against Guernsey for Jimmy Hill's Football Weekly touring XI

Channel Islands 1964 - 65

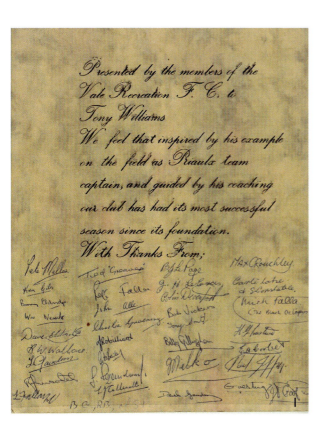

Sport may have an "agent" in England

GUERNSEY football, and possibly local sport as a whole, may soon have an official public relations officer — or "agent" — in England, writes Rex Bennet.

The G.F.A. have provisionally accepted an offer from Tony Williams, the former St Martin's, Vale Rec. and Island player and ex-Vale coach, who is now a freelance sports journalist and an executive of Ascot Promotions, to act in that capacity for them.

Mr Williams has had discussions with G.F.A. officials and with members of the States Tourist Committee during the past week and it is possible he may be invited by the committee to act not only for football but for Guernsey sport as a whole.

Memories Revived From Guernsey Sport

'While our Sylvans were brushing aside Blackfield & Langley in the Hampshire Senior Cup last Saturday, - well done, lads - Jersey's First Tower were winning just as comfortably in the FA Challenge Vase.

Also playing at home, Tower beat Hungerford Town 3-0 with two goals by big Mike Steigenberger and an absolute cracker by the not-so-big Simon Petullo.

Jersey's St.Peter, meantime were losing out 3-2 to Stoke Gabriel, in England in the Devon Premier Cup.

The fact that Tower were playing Hungerfod revived memories, for me, of that club paying visits to Guernsey when Tony Williams was their boss and of the Rothmans CI XI's great 4-2 win over the Hellenic League on the Town's ground back in 1977.

It also reminded me that Peter Blondel had had a season with Hungerford and that Tony Williams, the former St. Martin's, Vale Rec and Island forward and one time Vale manager, always claimed he was a triple international in that he had been capped by England (at youth level), Guernsey and The Isle of Man!

It was, of course, Williams who was instrumental in converting Vale Rec. from 'also rans' into one of our top clubs when he took them over in the mid-60's and persuaded several leading players to move to the Corbet Field with him.'

1. Thank you letter

2. Cutting from the Guernsey Sport

3. Three of the 1965 Muratti side that joined Vale Rec.
   Noel Jefferies, TW & Bonny Eldridge

Channel Islands 1964 - 65

Old friend and football colleague Bonny Eldridge *(back row left)* sent me a newspaper article **(below)** from Guernsey in December 2017, in which local Sports Editor Rob Batiste had suggested their struggling Belgraves Football Club ought to be strengthened by some senior players, rather then just continually struggle at the foot of the table.

Bonny and I had enjoyed re-building Vale Recreation in the same way in the 1965-1966 season and apparently Rob Baptiste also remembered that very exciting campaign. But I was never a 'flying winger', although I had worn No11 for Guernsey!

> 'It is called "Doing a Williams", senior players rallying to the rescue for one final challenge at the end of a career that has rewarded them so much. That – surely – would be more satisfying to the man who's won everything, than cruising through on automatic at one of the current big three'

'Doing a Williams' originates back in the mid-sixties when Vale Rec were suddenly sprung from no-hopers to trophy challengers by the vision of man who had quickly won everything in the Guernsey and CI game and thought "You know, how boring is this?"

Tony Williams was his name, a flying winger who arrived from the UK, immediately snapped up by the Saints as the only viable side to play for, and helped propel them to another set of cups. He could see it was not a challenge and so set out on one, targeting a group of players he knew well - many of them mainlanders - who wanted to make the Priaulx League a competition in more than name only. To a degree, Williams was almost immediately successful.

His very first year - 1965-66 - Rec landed the Stranger and made the Jeremie final. They made another Jeremie final in 1969 and seriously tested Saints dominance each year until, in 1972 -73, they finally got their hands on the Priaulx. By then, Williams was long gone to a new challenge in editing publications such as the Rothmans Football Annual, and most of those he brought along to the Corbet Field had gone too.

But the job had been done. The switch had been flicked. Combined with a well-ordered youth development programme that was to yield a long list of Muratti stars, Vale had become fashionable and noted, just as Bels can again quite easily. I laugh at the suggestion that Bels have brought their current predicament upon themselves, so why the lament ?

Easy answer to that: Because they did little to deserve it and with their youth situation are close to being beyond help. Half-a-century ago Williams quickly concluded that a real challenge can be hugely satisfying and Guernsey football was all the better for it.

by Sports Editor Rob Batiste

Guernsey United

**Footballers would benefit from playing in the UK if they are dedicated.
A former Muratti player who works closely with the FA's Competition would be able to help any moves for an Island team to enter a UK League.**

Nick Mollet of the Guernsey Press speaks to Tony Williams (15th January 2008)

The creation of a Guernsey United Football team to play in a national league is workable insists non-league expert and writer Tony Williams.

It's an exciting and sensible idea and would be great, provided the players are prepared to dedicate themselves to playing at least once a week. It would be really good for the players to get into national leagues. It's certainly workable and I would be willing to help if needed, he said.

Williams, the author of the Non-League Football Directory for the past 30 years, has an in depth knowledge of the Non-League game, believes if Guernsey were to go down this route, they might have to start by playing in the Hampshire League and this would entail midweek games.

'If the club gets onto the pyramid there is a chance of progressing into senior leagues and visiting exciting new grounds. But unless you sit around a table and have some prolonged discussions you will never know. You have to have ideas and speak to people who have experienced it and know about different options. You have to be open minded.

Even players living in the UK could perhaps play for a Guernsey United side. It's definitely worth pursuing - as its all conjecture and ifs and buts at this time'.

He cites the example of Truro City from Cornwall to demonstrate what would be achieved by rising up the Non-League ladder.

'If you are an outstanding side like Truro City, you will enjoy making progress and there is always the chance of sampling the thrills of qualifying for a match at Wembley.'

He explained that Guernsey would have to negotiate with The FA Competitions Committee regarding their most suitable League to join geographically.

'Guernsey people will have to realise that getting in won't be particularly easy, and there may be meetings needed where advice can be given by the FA. Whoever is organising the project in Guernsey would also have to realise how much time would be taken up and what sort of budget should be available to cover increased costs. There would have to be a lot of negotiations before it happens. Crowds and, in some cases facilities, in English local leagues are not as good as in Guernsey.'

Williams said that from the Island Senior competitions perspective, The Priaux League representative team had fared well in The FA National Systems Cup and had impressed by their general play and set piece routines.

'The best players in the island would form a formidable side. But they would have to be dedicated and fully committed to the team over a long season. You have to really care and really want to take on the challenge of senior football with more games and more travelling'

He insists a Guernsey United side could work, if the finances were in place and it did not ruin the clubs in the island and they were happy with the idea. It would be exhausting for any player to attempt to play and train within club football on the island and for Guernsey United.

He believes it is correct to be ambitious and look to the future but players competing in the Priaux league against the same clubs year after year must lose their spark, but this would not apply playing in a National League.

Returning to London from Guernsey couldn't have been timed any better, World Cup fever had begun to take over as the country was proudly preparing to host the 1966 World Cup.

With Roger Hunt a prominent member of Alf Ramsey's England squad I thought I would write and find out if it was him I had played alongside for the FA XI v London University. He confirmed it was him and he had featured in the photo in The Times, and suggested we should meet when the England team came to London for their next match.

The England team were training at Hendon so we met and have remained friends ever since. I was also helping at The Football Association at the time, and as some of the World Cup duties were distributed to staff and helpers and I was allocated a place in the team of crowd stewards at Wembley for a number of games including the final.

The atmosphere at Wembley for England's World Cup triumph could never be forgotten and my steward's patch was half way up the stand behind a corner flag. This meant I had a view through the side netting and right along the goal line in the goalmouth where England's disputed goal was scored off the crossbar by Geoff Hurst.

The ball was driven against the underside of the crossbar and, looking through the side netting, I saw the ball in the air well over the line and started to celebrate. However the spin after hitting the underside of the crossbar took the ball in an arc, and bounced back on the goal line.

I was one of the few people who actually knew the whole ball had crossed the goal line in the air and I couldn't understand what all the fuss was about.

Luckily the linesman had a similar view to me and the famous goal was the second in Geoff Hurst's memorable hat trick.

The atmosphere in London, and indeed throughout the Country, has never been matched and it was a day that every English football fan will remember for the rest of their lives.

Epsom & Ewell 1966 - 67

This little Surrey club will always be special to me as I enjoyed a spell as player manager with them in the sixties. It was a traumatic but thoroughly enjoyable and worthwhile experience although our pitch on the side of a hill in West Street did give us a big advantage!

I was not impressed by the father and son Chairman and Club Secretary who failed to warn me the club were awaiting punishment for too many red and yellow cards. After a couple of games suspension we returned to Athenian League matches and a visit to Wingate & Finchley. The local press described the game as a meeting between 'Rabbis and Vicars'. Under the new management Epsom & Ewell received no more bookings that season!

It was my first experience as club manager in senior amateur football and I had to rely on my contacts in the RAF or Old Boys football to strengthen our playing strength. The league position was looking severe when I took over, but we managed to pull away from the danger zone thanks to long serving John McNaught, John Wood and excellent strikers Ted Stafford and Jan Illasewicz.

The club was formed at the end of the First Word War and in 1924 joined the Surrey Senior League:

Surrey Senior League	1924 - 1927
London League	1927 - 1949
Corinthian League	1949 - 1963
Athenian League	1963 - 1973
Surrey Senior League	1973 - 1975
Athenian League	1975 - 1977
Isthmian League	1977 - 2006
Combined Counties League	2006 -

Some quality seasons were enjoyed at the turn of the century in The Isthmian League under the guidance of long serving manager Adrian Hill. However, the highlight of the club's history were the Wembley appearance in the first ever FA Vase Final in 1975, the Division Two championship in 1978 and the two top three finishes in Division One, which led to promotion in 1984.

It would be good to see Epsom & Ewell competing in a Step Four competition again and the club is determined to consistently challenge for promotion.

	P	W	D	L	F	A	Pts	Position
Epsom & Ewell First Half of the Season 1966-967	15	2	2	11	29	56	6	16
Season Record Second half	15	7	4	4	36	35	18	5
Final Statistics	30	9	6	15	65	91	24	12

The best results of the season were achieved against the champions Eastbourne United H 5-2 A 0-0

The third highest scoring league club with 65

Epsom & Ewell 1966 - 67

1. Epsom Lads

2. A valuable goal at home for the manager.

3. Giant centre forward Ted Stafford challenges for a cross

4. Epsom & Ewell 66-67

The Amateur Footballer

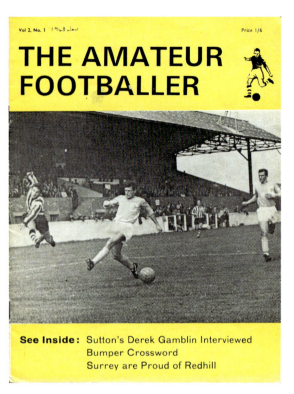

1. The Amateur Footballer

2. Greg Tesser chats to Tottenham Hotspur and Scotland star Dave Mackay

3. *From left to right:* The Wealdstone manager Vince Burgess with players Tony Slade, Tony McGuiness nd Hugh Lindsay

4. *From left to Right*
Peter Gleeson (Dulwich Hamlet manager) TW (Assoc Editor of The TAF) Gregory R. Tessor (Managing Editor of the TAF) Led Adam (Assoc Ed of Jimmy Hill's Football Weekly) Dave Swain (Weldstone) Chris Davies (Ed JH's FW)

Jimmy Hill 1967 - 1970

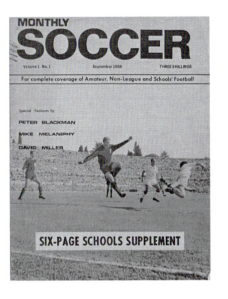

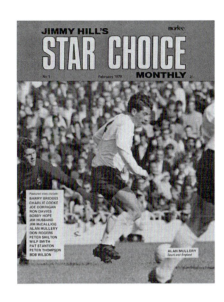

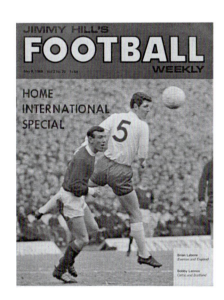
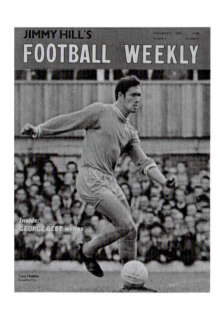

Thank to Jimmy Hill's enthusiasm and support

Jimmy Hill 1967 - 1970

While coaching and playing at Epsom I was also working for the excellent Office Cleaning Company and helping Greg Tesser with his Amateur Footballer magazine. But I was lucky to notice an advertisement for an Editor to look after 'Jimmy Hill's Football Weekly,' a relatively new football publication in 1967. It was a wonderful opportunity to work within the sport I loved and for someone highly respected in the game.

So a chance to meet Jimmy Hill who had created a unique reputation throughout the game would be a wonderful experience, from which I might get some advice from the great man, even if I was unsuitable for the job.

I had thoroughly enjoyed helping Greg Tesser with his Amateur Footballer magazine, but I was a rookie as far as journalism or magazine production was concerned. However, Jimmy was apparently pleased with my football record at Malvern College and considered I could be moulded into 'editorial shape' for 'Jimmy Hill's Football Weekly' in 1967

I looked forward every week to my early Monday morning meetings to decide the weeks editorial plan with Jimmy, who was the figurehead but not the owner of the publishing company. In fact the owners of the company publishing our magazines were not experienced or, as it proved, not too keen on sport. So it wasn't the easiest working relationship, but we just had to make the best of the situation.

Jimmy was extremely busy within the high powered world of sport but was always positive and helpful, whatever the situation. When the Second Yearbook justifiably received some bad publicity and the publishers signed up another editor, I'm sure it was Jimmy's recommendation that persuaded Rothmans to add me to their Marketing team to help promote all their sporting interests.

So thanks to Jimmy Hill, the man who had abolished the maximum wage for footballers, had built Coventry City into a leading British club, and was regarded as the most talented football executive in the country, I was starting a career marketing cigarettes, as a non-smoker!

After settling into this marketing job, I had wondered whether Rothmans might like to help the Hellenic League, the home of Hungerford Town. I had met their very enthusiastic chairman Norman Matthews, and thought I might be able to arrange some local support as their brands, Rothmans Kingsize, Piccadilly, Dunhill and Peter Stuyvesant had all been involved with sports in the past.

I had mentioned the idea to Norman Matthews and had also discussed the possibility with Doug Insole, the famous Essex and England cricketer, whom I had met when playing in the same forward line for Corinthian-Casuals.

Unknown to me, Doug and Jimmy Hill had already discussed the possibility of a company sponsoring a football league. Their ideas developed into a wonderful scheme that would promote successful sporting football. Using me as an executive already in the company, and as someone they knew to be a dedicated football person, they accepted that Rothmans, experienced in sports sponsorship, might be an ideal choice.

With Doug involved with The Isthmian League and knowing that their chairman Barry East was also looking for a sponsorship scheme for his famous competition, they were the obvious first choice with The Hellenic League also accepted, as Norman Matthews had already also shown his enthusiasm for the idea.

Jimmy Hill 1967 - 1970

The Western League (Division One), plus The Guernsey and Jersey Leagues were also added, as was the famous Northern League the following year.

So Jimmy Hill and Doug Insole presented the first ever sponsorship scheme for football leagues, to be contested over a full season.

The majority of clubs improved their attitudes, qualified for prize money and as referees enjoyed their matches so much more without dissent and, inspired by the occasional smile, football became a much more enjoyable occupation for all concerned.

The well behaved clubs also strangely did well in cup ties against clubs still 'out of control'.

Thanks to Jimmy Hill and Doug Insole sponsorship became a necessity for every league and still is. The Premier League being the most famous example to the rest of the world. But do they play with a smile?

Jimmy Hill was probably the most brilliant football personality in the history of the English game and, with Doug Insole's help on this occasion, they probably ensured that every football league in the world will continue to enjoy sponsorship in one form or another. It was a privilege to work with both of them.

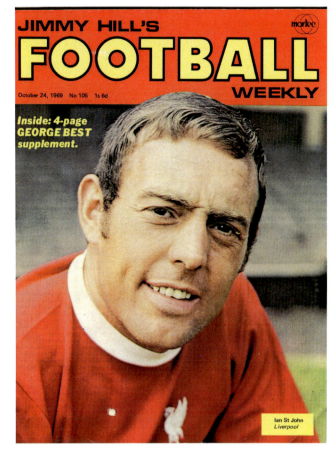

The Football Weekly editorial team includes great friend Peter Grove (behind me), Ken Adam (Assistant Editor) behind my lovely wife Hillary (in white).

Opposite : Centre spread from Jimmy Hill's Weekly

Jimmy Hill 1967 - 1970

A page from Jimmy Hill's Weekly

1970 - 1986

Rothmans Launch

Creating the Rothmans Football Yearbook

Publishing sports magazines brought introductions to the production and distribution sides of the business and there was no doubt that the people with most knowledge of the trade were those I had met at WH Smith. The famous book shop had branches all over the country but in their head office, senior heads of department really knew their business.

At a meeting with their magazine buyers I asked their advice about an idea I had for a book and was introduced to the head of the sports books department. It was soon obvious he knew what type of book was popular, what price was sensible, where in the country sales would be best and how many copies their branches were likely to sell.

Wisdens of Football

I explained that I had an idea for a 'Wisdens' of Football. The reply was a little surprising! 'Unlike educated cricket supporters, football fans might have difficulty coping with a big book, surely they are better reading magazines and newspapers'. Despite our World Cup success in 1966, WH Smith had not considered serious books for the massive world of football supporters, but they accepted the challenge for the idea if I could find a sponsor to ensure we could cope with the extensive costs.

I discussed the idea with Roy Peskett, the senior football writer at The Daily Mail, who was coming to the end of a very successful career in Fleet Street. He was enthusiastic about the idea and another great contact was Geoff Irvine, a Malvern College football team mate, who had got a football 'blue' at Oxford and was working with Bagenal Harvey, the top sports agent in the country who was also looking after Jimmy Hill's sporting contracts.

They all liked the idea, and as Bagenal's sports agency had handled some of Rothmans sporting sponsorships, which had proved to be very popular, he knew the people who might also like this project.

So The Football Yearbook for 1970-1971 was given the go ahead. It would be sponsored by Rothmans, published by Queen Anne Press and the copyright held by one of Bagenal Harvey's companies, Brickfield Publications Limited.

The first edition was encouraging, with the book receiving a great media welcome thanks to Bagenal Harvey's many contacts and encouragement from the Football Association.

The second year was a disaster. Most of my compiling was done without even a typewriter. My colleague Roy, was having a difficult time at the end of his career and was socialising a lot, and at the last important two weeks before supplying the finalised copy to the printer, the chairman of the publishing company had safely locked all our copy away in a special safe before leaving for a fortnight's holiday!

On his return there was neither the time nor the people available to prepare and check the copy and present it properly. I was understandably held responsible as the main driving force behind the project, but the book was a disaster with so many mistakes and emissions - the worst possible nightmare which produced terrible publicity and quite rightly the sack for the editors. Happily the Rothmans Football Yearbook (now sponsored by Sky) has gone from strength to strength thanks to excellent editors Jack Rollin and his daughter Glenda who have done a great job.

Every Cloud has a Silver Lining

As I was working as a freelance with a growing family after the closing down of Martec Publishing, it was a frightening situation, but happily it produced a silver lining. Was it a kind word from Jimmy Hill, Bagenal Harvey or Geoff Irvine? Or was it perhaps the Rothmans executives themselves, who had enjoyed the original idea and launch of the first Rothmans Football Yearbook?

Whoever it was, I was relieved to receive an invitation to join Carreras Rothmans Marketing Department!

The company was famous for its sponsorship of sport, with Dunhill involved with Show Jumping, Peter Stuyvescent Sailing, Piccadilly Golf and Rothmans Cricket and Tennis so it looked like a perfect job apart from the fact I didn't smoke!

Through The Rothmans Yearbook I had met most of the Rothmans marketing team. They knew the first book was initially popular but the second edition had been a disappointment in many ways, but after initial doubting, WH Smith were apparently prepared to back the idea providing the book had a sponsor.

Rothmans Football Yearbook

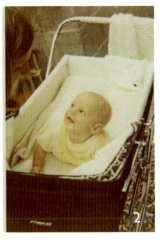

Opposite: Wedding day with Hilary June 1969

1. A happy family in a new home in Great Bedwyn where statistics for the Rothmans Football Yearbook were completed

2. Michael celebrating his first Mother's Day

3. The Donnington Village team - my last football club as player

4. The Rothmans Football yearbook foreword written by FIFA President Stanley Rous

5. Rothmans publicity Sports Minister Denis Howell, Matt Busby and Jimmy Hill in front of the Coach and Horses.

Examples of general press reaction to our new publication

Football's Wisden

At last British football has its Wisden - a comprehensive reference book on the game. It costs 18s, but contains 992 pages and is produced annually. The first issue names an ideal Great Britain team:

Gordon Banks, David Hay, Mike England, Bobby Moore, Terry Cooper, Billy Bremmer, Alan Ball, Jimmy Johnstone, Geoff Hurst, Ron Davies and George Best.

* *Rothmans Football Yearbook 1970/71 Queen Anne Press*

A Record Book with Everything

Fans love picking sides to represent Great Britain and the Soccer writers are no different. In the new Rothmans Football Yearbook 1970-71, 22 well known journalists have selected the following team for Rothmans Golden Boots Award.

Great Britain (40204 formation): Gordon Banks, David Hay, Mike England, Bobby Moore, Terry Cooper, Billy Bremmer, Alan Ball, Jimmy Johnstone, Geoff Hurst, Ron Davies and George Best.

Players with the next highest number of votes were Martin Peters, Billy McNeil and Francis Lee. This is just one of the many fascinating features in this book, which must now be regarded as the Soccer fan's Wisden.

Nearly 1,000 pages thick, this book has everything. Career records of goals, League appearances, internationals and all the facts about the 92 League clubs.

Tabulated records of every League table, all the line-ups, results and goalscorers last season, plus every League result since the war. And, of course, there is a similar section deal with Scottish cubs.

Rothmans have put all that Soccer fans could possibly want to know in one book - European competitions, F.A.Cup records, amateur and sponsored football.

As Sir Stanley Rous says in his foreword: "I do not remember seeing a book of similar quality about Association Football."

Presenting - the Wisden of Soccer

When was the goalkeeper's use of hands restricted to the penalty area?
Who figured in the first £1000 football transfer?
What vital piece of equipment was invented by Mr Brodie?
How many clubs played in Division II in season 1892 - 93?
The answers to these and a million other soccer queries can be found in the first Rothmans Football Yearbook.

Although Rothmans 992 pages fall 98 pages short of this summer's Wisden, it is the nearest football has approached the cricket's 'bible'.

For detailed, authoritative and concise references to almost any subject, this is the most revealing and enjoyable work so far. If you are a Channel Islands Marquis League fan, look up pages 873. Or the 1900 Paris Olympics on page 805, or the European Cup or the FA Cup or League Championship or career goalscorer or ....

It is crammed with information - all worthwhile, all immensely readable. Every grade of the game receives healthy mention, from the English Schools Trophy through to the amateur and professional ranks of the World Cup.

Counterpart to Wisden

Football has, until this week, had no real equivalent of cricket's Wisden. With a century of tradition to command its authority, Wisden sets a high standard, but the 992 page Rothmans Yearbook, published by Queen Anne Press at 18s, is already a presentable counterpart, writes Norman Fox.

Tony Williams and Roy Peskett, who compiled the book, claim it is the most comprehensive reference book in Association Football. Invaluable to the professional writer or amateur statistician, the yearbook sets out all the usual records but in greater detail than can be found elsewhere. With greater emphasis on European football, which is lacking in literature, and an index, this can become the standard textbook on the national game.

A variety of reviews for the first edition of the Rothmans Football Yearbook

Launch of the Rothmans Football Yearbook

1. Eusebio, Sports Minister Denis Howell, Rothmans official and Bobby Moore

2. Matt Busby, Rothmans Director, Denis Howell and editor

3. Rothmans Good News Awards were framed paintings by Daily Express cartoonist Roy Ullyett. Geoffery Green, senior football journalist of 'The Times' receives his award

4. Rothmans executive John Lander and the editor present Emlyn Hughes with his award

5. Lunch at The Launch, Jimmy Hill, Tony Williams .Ted Croker (FA Chief Exec)& Don Revie

6. A team of retired International stars

Rothmans Introduce the First Ever Sponsorship of Football Leagues

A meeting was arranged with Michael Lock, The Marketing Chairman at Baker Street, which I will never forget. Although a non-smoker, I thought that perhaps I should attempt to puff on a Rothmans Kingsize to show willing, so I managed to light up, but being a bundle of nerves, I put the burning end on my lips!

I think this got me an offer of work as the chairman couldn't stop laughing, so I was excited to have the chance to join their marketing team. At the time, John King was in charge of the company's sports sponsorship which included some very popular and successful contracts. He was a charismatic and very successful leader who knew his sport and the company brands.

Promoting sales of cigarettes was a job, but obviously I couldn't really put my heart and soul into my work as a non-smoker. I had to find some different aspect of the work on which I could really associate myself with enthusiasm. The great news however, was the inclusion of a company car within my contract and living in Great Bedwyn just over the Wiltshire border, I really appreciated it. The fact that the Marketing Department of the famous cigarette company had been so successful with their involvement in sport, enabled me to suggest possible sponsorship for local football leagues and to receive reasonable encouragement and positive help from head office.

While assisting manager Dennis Giles with a bit of coaching at Hungerford Town, I had come in contact with The Hellenic League led by a very enthusiastic Secretary, Norman Matthews who had been a Football League referee. He had wondered whether the Rothmans budget would stretch to the Berks, Bucks and Oxford area for a bit of help for his Football League. This gave me some ideas that perhaps John King might be prepared to consider inviting other leagues to benefit from the Rothmans sporting budget.

The Rothmans Football League Sponsorship
Having persuaded the regional budget holder to offer some modest incentives to their local Hellenic Football League, the gratitude shown by League Secretary Norman Matthews made me realise the potential within the major winter sport throughout the country.

At the same time, Isthmian Chairman Barry East who had already enjoyed great success at his Leytonstone club, was considering sponsorship seriously and asked his East London friend, the famous England and Essex cricketer and Pegasus and Corinthian Casuals winger Doug Insole, to think about the idea.

Doug contacted my ex boss, Jimmy Hill, the top sports marketing entrepreneur of the time, and they drew up a wonderful presentation recommending sponsorship for a football league to encourage and promote sporting, attractive and successful football.

I was lucky to have been in the right place at the right time once again, thanks to my experience with 'Jimmy Hill's Weekly', playing with Corinthian Casuals in the same forward line as Doug Insole and of course getting to know Rothmans through the Football Yearbook.

I was asked to introduce the sponsorship package, drawn up by Jimmy and Doug, to the marketing department at Rothmans. The traditional Sales Force of the cigarette company also needed some persuasion to accept that a spectacular football sponsorship could be an advantage for them out on the road.

The suggested prize money for successful clubs and the incentives for sportsmanship for the four leagues, with two divisions each, added up to about £95,000 and when there was a nasty silence after my presentation, I feared the worst.

'I think you've made a mistake with your calculations. A sponsor should be seen to be successful by the public and everyone involved, so extra money is needed to promote all that we are hoping to do to help the sport. No, you need at least £150,000 to do this, so come back with some ideas of how you can tell the world its Rothmans sponsoring the Isthmian, Hellenic, Northern and Western Leagues. It's a great idea but let's do it properly!'

As Barry East had been one of the original promoters of the idea that football could be sponsored, the famous Isthmian League deserved to be involved, and as Norman Matthews the Hellenic League's leader had already also sampled a little local support from Rothmans, it was accepted that The Isthmian and Hellenic Leagues should be offered sponsorship for the 1973-1974 season.

Not surprisingly, both leagues agreed to become football sponsorship pioneers and Doug and Jimmy had already drawn up the awards based on results and sportsmanship that included wonderful rewards and incentives. The Rothmans marketing department then had to suggest the budgets that could be made available for two more regional leagues.

John King, the Sports Marketing boss was obviously very supportive, but it was up to him to motivate the senior salesmen and also get advice on which geographical areas would benefit most from local football sponsorship by Carreras Rothmans. Clubs in the original two leagues would be ideal for Rothmans as they covered the home counties, but after much discussion, it was decided that two other areas should be invited and perhaps Carreras Rothmans would benefit most from involvement in the West Country and The North East.

So, after the success and encouraging publicity created by The Rothmans Isthmian and Rothmans Hellenic Leagues, the officials of the Northern and Western Football leagues were happy to accept invitations to form a quartet of sponsored semi-professional competitions in the 1974-1975 season.

My job, having a football background, would be to administer the whole sponsorship on a day to day basis, but firstly the Marketing Director would have to give the go ahead and decide upon a suitable budget.

Rothmans Introduce the First **Ever** Sponsorship of Football Leagues

ROTHMANS SPONSORSHIP SCHEME FOR NON-LEAGUE FOOTBALL

BASIC PRINCIPLES

1. ATTACKING FOOTBALL

    The points system in both Divisions of the League to be changed so that three points are given for a win and only one for a draw.

    Clubs are not so likely to play for a draw as one win is now worth three draws. Away clubs tend to attack very much more than their counterparts in leagues where a victory is only worth two points.

2. GOAL INCENTIVES

    a) Weekly Awards

    If a club wins a match by three clear goals, i.e. either 4-1, 3-0, etc., it will be paid a bonus of £40.

    If a club is winning by two goals they are encouraged to push for a third to qualify for a bonus. With this in mind 'playing for time' is practically eliminated and the game remains a better spectacle right to the final whistle.

    b) Season Awards

    These awards will apply to the three highest scoring clubs who have not received a cash prize for finishing first, second, or third in their respective divisions.

    Clubs out of the running for championship or promotional places near the end of the season can still have a 'cause' by going for goals and qualifying as one of the leading goalscorers.

3. SPORTSMANSHIP POOL

    Teams will lose four points if a player is sent off, and one if he is cautioned. If a team loses eight points or more in the course of a season, it will not qualify for a share of the Sportsmanship Pool. Teams who qualify to share the Pool i.e. by not accumulating eight points against them, will receive a pro rata share of the Pool according to the number of points lost. This scale will be carefully devised so that it is understood by all clubs at the outset.

4. INCENTIVES TO WIN THE LEAGUE

    The incentives for 1st, 2nd and 3rd place will be as shown on the list of basic sponsorship awards but if a team finishes 1st, 2nd or 3rd it loses eight disciplinary points on the scale set out above, i.e. four points for a sending off and one for a caution, and it will not qualify for the prize money. The money instead will go towards increasing the Sportsmanship Pool in its Division. The above will also apply to the Seasons Awards for goal incentives.

This was the original official paperwork regarding The Rothmans Football League sponsorship as discussed and accepted.

Rothmans Introduce the First **Ever** Sponsorship of Football Leagues

BASIC SPONSORSHIP AWARDS
FOR
ROTHMANS FOOTBALL LEAGUES
SEASON 1976-77

Prize Money	Champions	Second	Third
Division 1 R.I.L. North & West (Premier Division)	£1,000	£500	£300
Division 2 R.I.L.	£600	£300	£200
Division 3 R.I.L.	£500	£250	£150
Rothmans Hellenic League	£500	£200	
Rothmans Western League (Division One)	£400	£150	
Rothmans Jersey Football Combination	£300		
Rothmans Priaulx League (Guernsey)	£200	£100	

Clubs with most goals in a season who do not win League prize money

	Highest Scorers	Second Highest	Third Highest
Division 1 R.I.L. North & West (Premier Division)	£300	£200	£100
Division 2 R.I.L.	£200	£120	£60
Division 3 R.I.L.	£150	£100	£50
Rothmans Hellenic League	£150	£100	
Rothmans Western League (Division One)	£125	£75	
Rothmans Jersey Football Combination	£100		
Rothmans Guernsey Priaulx	£100		

Sportsmanship Pool

Division 1 R.I.L. Northern & Western (Premier Division)	£2,000
Division 2 R.I.L.	£1,000
Rothmans Hellenic League, Division 3 R.I.L.	£1,000
Rothmans Western League (Division One)	£750
Rothmans Jersey Combination	£500
Rothmans Guernsey Priaulx League	£500

Teams will lose four points if a player is sent off, and one point if a player is cautioned. If a team loses 8 points or more in the course of a season it will not qualify for a share of the Sportsmanship Pool or prize money as shown above.

Match by Match Incentives - Victories by Three Clear Goals

Division 1 R.I.L. Northern & Western (Premier Division)	£40
Division 2 R.I.L.	£25
Rothmans Hellenic League, Division 3 R.I.L.	£20
Rothmans Western League (Division One)	£17.50
Rothmans Jersey Football Combination and Rothmans Guernsey Priaulx League	£10

Three points are awarded for a win, and one for a draw in all sponsored leagues.

The FIRST to be Sponsored and the FIRST to reward victories with three points. were:-

The Rothmans Leagues
The Isthmian and Hellenic Leagues in 1973-1974
plus The Northern and Western Leagues in 1974-1975

Rothmans Introduce the First Sponsorship of Football Leagues

1. The Isthmian League announce the Rothmans Sponsorship.

2. Western League chairman Les Phillips with Jimmy Hill, Joe Mercer and Ted Croker.

3. The Rothmans Hellenic League local publicity

4. Famous International Referee Jim Finney, supported by the Rothmans sales girls, at a Rothmans Western League five a side competition at Plymouth.

5. Northern League welcomes Rothmans

6. The First Rothmans News

7. Rothmans Awards Lunch

Rothmans Introduce the First **Ever** Sponsorship of Football Leagues

ISTHMIAN LEAGUES 1977-78

Awards as they would have been under the Rothmans Sponsorship

Three Divisions (22+22+17) = 61 clubs

BASIC AWARDS

	Championship	Second	Third	
Division One	1,000	500	300	(1,800)
Division Two	600	300	200	(1,100)
Division Three	500	250	150	(900)
				£3,800

Clubs with most goals in a season who do not win League prize money

	Highest Scorers	Second Highest	Third Highest	
Division One	300	200	100	(600)
Division Two	200	120	60	(380)
Division Three	150	100	50	(300)
				£1,280

Sportsmanship Pool

Division One	2,000
Division Two	1,000
Division Three	1,000
	£4,000

MATCH BY MATCH INCENTIVES

(Victories by Three Goals)

	PER MATCH	ESTIMATED TOTAL PER SEASON
Division One	£40	3,200
Division Two	£20	1,750
Division Three	£20	1,500
Total		6,450

General League Administration

Donation towards match officials fees	2,000
League Representative Matches League Presentation Dinner League Handbook League Bulletins League Officers Expenses, Stationery etc.	2,470
Total Expenditure	£20,000

Rothmans Sponsorship Scheme

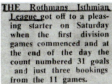

1. Rod Haider receives a blown up photo of his famous FA Cup goal that earned Rothmans Isthmian club Hendon an FA Cup replay at Newcastle.

2. Rothmans enjoyed good press coverage

3. A special gift from Rothmans to the Jersey FA on their special anniversary

4. Rothmans on Tour in The Canary Islands

5. Coach Jim Kelman with Famous Guest Player, Geoff Hurst

Rothmans Sponsorship Scheme

The Marketing Director's challenge opened up all sorts of ideas but we started by asking the art department for a suitable football sponsorship logo. Something we could link with all publications likely to publicise Rothmans League results, league tables and of course the brilliant Jimmy Hill and Doug Insole sportsmanship scheme.

The promotional and financial back up encouraged by the Marketing department gave the whole operation wonderful character. Magazines, annuals, car stickers, magnetic result boards for club houses and match advertising boards for outside grounds all including the football logo. So it wasn't long before we got the go ahead to publish monthly magazines to keep the football world up to date with our leagues' progress and sponsorship news including the popular sportsmanship awards.

To round up the year's sponsored football we introduced annuals to follow the monthly magazines and then to publicise the progress made and alert Rothmans overseas contacts, end of seasons tours were arranged. The Channels Islands had also been introduced to The Rothmans Football 'Family' which was obviously particularly exciting for me after the happy two years that I had spent in Guernsey.

What a wonderful job! Publicising Non-League football with a famous company's backing and realising that everyone - the company, the clubs, the media, football in general and of course myself, were all benefiting and enjoying a really positive and exciting promotion.

Probably the most exciting project was the tour to the Canary Islands with a squad I could select from the Rothmans leagues and helped by the Hungerford coach Jimmy Kelman and celebrity guest Geoff Hurst, our World Cup hat trick man. What a dream! Each League sent a Committee man and we were looked after by the Rothmans executives on the Islands. The lads represented Rothmans socially in their smart touring blazers and trained hard but still found time for some memorable socialising!

The sponsored clubs even improved their cup results, as officials quite naturally preferred disciplined players to those full of abuse and aggression. So difficult decisions often appeared to go their way! Even the bonding was enjoyed between sponsored league clubs and their administrators, through inter league representative games, overseas tours and The Rothmans National Cup in which teams from all four leagues competed against each other.

For five years all the good aspects of Non-League football were appreciated and enjoyed by the Rothmans Leagues, their member clubs and their supporters.

Sadly, Britain's entry into the Common Market brought a change of policy to the Cigarette company relying on sales of their king size cigarettes, so to keep their products and prices competitive, all involvement with sports sponsorship was curtailed.

Carreras Rothmans cigarette company had shown the advantages of league sponsorship, and it helped to promote the best aspects of our national game i.e attacking play, discipline and general sportsmanship.

There is no doubt that the leadership of Rothmans and their four leagues, working to the wonderfully simple but productive incentives, provided all that was good in the game.

Before the end of the Rothmans Football involvement, I was particularly pleased that the Channel Islands leagues in Guernsey and Jersey joined the 'family', with their clubs also entering the cups and of course welcoming touring sides.

> The rest of the country have followed the Rothmans example and now every league expects to have a sponsor. Sadly, they don't necessarily promote the same sporting and positive principles introduced for Rothmans by Doug Insole and Jimmy Hill, who were dedicated and brilliant sportsmen in their own right. They had known exactly how to produce the incentives to encourage entertaining and sporting football and not many other leagues, or their sponsors, have since enjoyed similar advice and professional sporting knowledge.

The Football League obviously jumped on the bandwagon and the senior competition has attracted immense financial rewards through television coverage. The Premier League emerged and has become the world's most attractive and wealthy sponsored football league!

Its no wonder that Rothmans were so pleased with their pioneering sponsorship of football leagues, as they received press coverage like this throughout the Home Counties (featuring The Isthmian & Hellenic Leagues), the West Country (Western League) and The North East (Northern League).

It's also not surprising that every modern league, at every level, now expect to attract sponsors. The game's leagues and clubs have never had so much money. But they also have more pressure on them to use it properly.

Rothmans Sponsorship Scheme

When summing up their five years of Rothmans sponsorship, The Isthmian League Centenary book noted that:-
'everyone involved in this sponsorship seemed to benefit'

* **The Leagues** and their clubs had an extra source of income.

* **The sponsors** experienced a tremendous boost in sales in all areas covering their four regional leagues with record numbers of new accounts opened. Plus many more mentions in the national and local press.

* **The media** actually appeared to approve, giving the sponsors the massive coverage that a cigarette company had never before experienced. The brilliant system of awards set up by Doug Insole and Jimmy Hill, actually achieved their aim to produce more attacking football and a higher level of sportsmanship. In fact Blyth Spartans, the pride of the North East, actually won a Northern League title without a single caution in one season and Wycombe Wanderers, the Isthmian Champions, achieved another championship with just one caution.

* **Match officials** enjoyed refereeing in the sponsored Leagues. Dissent was a rarity, players seemed to be competing with a smile and even the spectators enjoyed the atmosphere much more than the simmering aggression and dissent previously experienced.

When one considers these points, one realises how true that was and I also realised how lucky I was to have been involved in such a happy time for the game I love.

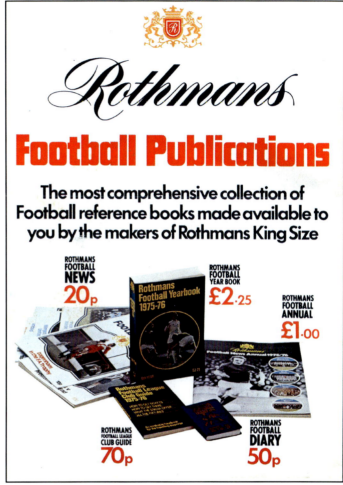

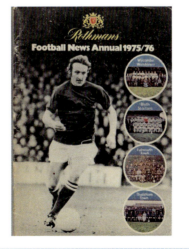

Hungerford Town in the Seventies

Having moved to Great Bedwyn, a little village just over the Berkshire/Wiltshire border, I met Dennis Giles, a lovely football enthusiast who had taken Hungerford Town up to the Premier Division of the Hellenic League and suggested I could help him as coach.

The Chairman was Ron Tarry who had played, coached, managed, looked after the ground and was prepared to help any schemes that would see his club develop on and off the field.

The club represented a fabulous little country town with a surprising amount of support and plenty of local football talent, stretching into Reading and Swindon. With my job becoming more and more involved with The Football Association, football publications and the Rothmans Sponsorship, I realised I had the contacts that could help the club develop.

A small club house and new changing rooms were officially opened with a game against World Cup and Liverpool hero Roger Hunt's All star XI. We were also accepted in the FA Cup for the first time in 1973-74 and lost at Southern League Trowbridge Town 2-4 after a 1-1 home draw. Extra seating and a clubhouse extension were officially opened by FA Secretary Ted Croker and a game against The England Amateur XI in the 1975-76 season

I enjoyed my role as General Manager and with well known local coaches George Pullen and Jimmy Kelman in charge of playing matters, the club were accepted by The Isthmian League. Friendlies were arranged against touring countries such as Saudi Arabia and Kuwait, who stayed at the local Health Hydro and also played international matches against Wales. A Summer Ball with 200 guests in a marquee on the ground received national publicity, as Jimmy Hill was involved in a car crash on his way to the event and finished up in a Reading hospital !

The full England squad also trained at Hungerford under Don Revie and the club's form with outstanding players such John Ashton, Ian Farr, David Ingram, Des McMahon, Norman Matthews Andy Wallace and Andy Young took Hungerford Town to three FA Vase Semi-Finals (1976, 1978 & 1980) and the First Round of the FA Cup (1979-1980).

The Rothmans Cup also gave the club some exiting trips to the North East where they were never on the losing side despite traveling to Crook Town, Guisborough, South Bank and Willington. Great fun, good experience and useful publicity! The Berks & Bucks Senior Cup Final was won at the fourth attempt but the development of the club can be gauged by The Hellenic League's letter of congratulations to the club secretary after Hungerford had beaten Wycombe Wanderers in a cup semi-final.

In 1979-1980 Hungerford Town reached the First Round Proper of the FA Cup with a 5-0 home victory in a replay against Southern League Bridgend, but wretched luck provided an away tie against old county rivals Slough Town instead of Portsmouth or Reading!

The highlight of the period however, must have been Hungerford Town's trip to represent the Isthmian League in the Anglo Italian Tournament.

Hungerford In Italy

Many of the original games between English and Italian clubs brought the worst behaviour out of our players who had been brainwashed by the football press over the years. They were led to believe that the Italians were petty, obstructive and ultra defensive on the field and not to be trusted with referees off it. Consequently it took time for our clubs to face their continental opponents in the right spirit.

Gigi Peronace, a famous Italian Football administrator based in London, was determined we should all get on well and eventually would understand each other and indeed the hospitality shown by most clubs was first class. I enjoyed the warmth of the Italian welcome personally as General Manager of Hungerford Town, when our little Berkshire club enjoyed the thrill of a football lifetime being selected by the Isthmian League to be one of their representatives in the 1981 Anglo Italian Tournament.

The Southern League and The Isthmian League had promised two clubs each to fill our quota of four English representatives. Each team would play two Italian clubs at home and two others away. Poole Town and Bridgend Town, the current Southern League Midland section Champions, who we had beaten 5-0 in the FA Cup in the previous season, represented the Southern League and Oxford City, under the managership of Bobby Moore, was the other Isthmian club. Alan Turvey with whom I had worked closely together in The Rothmans sponsorship days, suggested that Hungerford could help out by filling the second Isthmian slot, as the expenses of a weeks tour seemed to be prohibitive to most of his clubs.

His phone call came on a Saturday lunchtime just before we played Windsor & Eton in The FA Vase Fifth Round and I promised him we would fill the gap if we lost! We had reached the FA Vase Semi-Finals twice in the previous three years and obviously the club was determined to do even better, but our star goalscorer Ian Farr was at his brother's wedding and Windsor were a very good side at the time.

So straight after the game I was on the phone to Alan Turvey. We had lost the tie 0-1, but I didn't admit that the club committee didn't know I had accepted the Italian involvement on their behalf!

The total cost of the tour would be about £10,000 so the attitude of the small country town club's committee can be imagined when I broke the news that we had the honour and thrill of representing our town, our league and our country in The Anglo Italian Tournament!

Hungerford Town in the Seventies

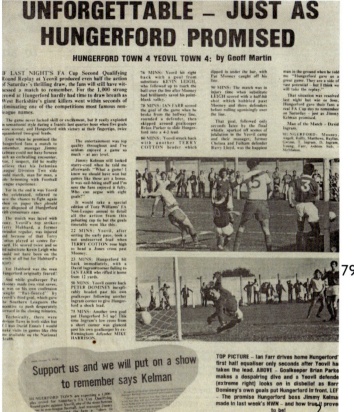

1. Ted Croker with Chairman Ron Tarry officially opens the clubhouse extention

2. HTFC 4 Yeovil T 4

3. Thanks to HTFC from Norman Matthews Secretary of The Hellenic League

4. Roger Hunt's XI celebrated the opening of Hungerford Town's first clubhouse.
   The team (in white) *included back row, left to right:* Harold Jarman, three Bristol City players, Jim Finney International Referee. Sitting: Bruce Walker, Gordon Milne (Liverpool & England), Roger Hunt (Liverpool & England World Cup 66) and Douggie Webb (Reading) *Front Row:* Micky Travers and David Johnson (Reading)

Hungerford Town in the Seventies

As general manager I took it upon myself to raise the money and the local businesses were brilliant. They rose to the occasion as they seemed to think the honour of representing England was worth supporting and Swindon Town even offered their ground for our first home game.

The match receipts for this game were not as substantial as we had hoped and a bad tempered game with S.S.Francavilla ended in a 3-3 draw. In fact the main memory was of the Italian manager presenting the referee with a present in the corridor outside his dressing room before the game!

Three days later the heavens opened and our support was limited to just over a hundred spectators who braved the weather to see us beat U.S.Civitanovese 1-0 with a goal from Joe Scott, our record signing from Yeovil Town.

So it was off to Italy with a win and a draw but unfortunately neither top scorer Ian Farr nor our new signing Joe Scott were available for what would surely be an historic and memorable tour for Hungerford Town Football Club.

The first stage of the tour very nearly was - for the wrong reasons! We travelled to the Italian South coast to the wonderful seaside resort of San Remo but the hotel facilities were not of a very high standard and we had made a very big mistake in allowing wives and girl friends to accompany the players on the tour. They showed their discontent which upset some of the players, who complained, and the situation annoyed the club and league officials, who were expecting everyone to make the best of a bad situation.

Ingram Whittington, the very popular Isthmian League Secretary was traveling with us and helped smooth over the niggles and we all enjoyed an afternoon on the beach, where veteran committee man Denis Giles admitted to a 'slight stirring' when walking across the beach strewn with topless beauties! The game itself was disappointing, but perhaps not surprising in the circumstances. We lost 1-3 and looked forward to a trip to the big city of Modena.

This was the famous home of the Alfa Romeo and also the Pannini book of football stickers! It was a complete change from San Remo and the hotel was excellent. An early evening drink at a pub across the road brought an interesting meeting with some opulent looking young men all of whom were enjoying soft drinks. They turned out to be Modena players who couldn't understand how our lads were allowed alcoholic drinks the day before a game!

The match was to be the warm up game before an Italian Under 23 International, so Hungerford in a very smart new all red kit were welcomed on to the pitch by a crowd of over 20,000 and before we had settled, were one down. With a superb display against a very good Italian Serie C club (National Third Division), the home team were restricted to just one more goal and as Modena went on to win the competition Final 4-1 against Poole, we considered our score respectable. As a bonus we were able to see a full colour recording of the whole game on television in all the pubs throughout the city that evening. It was difficult to believe it was really little Hungerford playing in Italy in front of such a massive crowd.

On returning, the local Sports Editor, Malcolm Howe gave us a full page in The Newbury Weekly News, which is on display in the current Hungerford Town Boardroom. This covered all aspects of the tour and there is no doubt that if all the English clubs, who had the luck to be involved with the Anglo Italian competitions, benefitted as much from the experience as The Hungerford Town club, then we all had a great deal for which to thank Gigi Peronace and the enthusiastic administrators from both countries.

Hungerford Town in the Seventies

Opposite: Our son Michael usually kicked a ball about behind the goal on a Hungerford matchday and looked the part in a tour shirt!

1. The Hungerford Town touring party in their new kit for the Italian trip.

2. Hungerford Town walk out for the club's second match, in front of 20,000 at Modena

3. The full England team trained at Hungerford's ground with Don Revie

4. The Italian trip begins in the coach from the ground

Hungerford Town in the Seventies

Hungerford's inspiration steps down

Tony Williams, whose inspiration set Hungerford off on a meteoric rise in the football world, has stepped down from the post as the club's General Manager. Mr. Williams has resigned for personal and business reasons after more than 10 years with the club. He gave his decision to club chairman Ron Tarry this week. Said Mr. Tarry 'We have no option but to allow Tony to stand down. We have to accept the situation, and we just hope that he will be able to come back some time in the future."

Business pressures have forced this action from Mr. Williams, who has served the club as coach, manager and general manager. The success of Rothmans Non-League annual, of which he is editor, means that he has to spend more time on compilation and promotion. The pressures of producing the book and running his own football promotions company had already cut down the amount of time he was able to spend with the club.

"To be honest, I have been doing less and less for the club over the last three or four years. It has got to the point when Hungerford can easily look after themselves, and now I have got to look after myself as well. I have had to examine my future and feel it is with the Non-League Annual. There is a big future for it, and my place is in promoting it, and that means at clubs up and down the country and I would not be able to devote proper time to the club. I have thoroughly enjoyed my years at Hungerford" said Mr Williams, "and everything is going well with the club and the team's potential looks excellent".

Mr. Williams, played for Corinthian Casuals, Grantham, Hereford and Bedford among others, also representing the RAF and FA XI. He was appointed coach under manager Dennis Giles in the summer of 1971, and his experience and contacts helped to establish Hungerford in the forefront of Non-League football.

"It has been hard work, but we are a senior club now and we have achieved what we set out to do" he said. "When I came to Hungerford, we had just won the Hellenic League's First Division and challenge cup under Dennis Giles. We went into the Premier Division, got back into the FA Amateur Cup, the FA Cup and the Vase. We got back into the Berks and Bucks Senior Cup, built lights and the club-house, and had matches against Maltese Falcons, Kuwait and Saudi Arabia, and went to Italy as well.

It has all been great fun and I am keen to support the club in whatever way possible, but I cannot afford to be tied. I am not 100% certain that I shall be staying in the area, as my work may force me to move back to London. My business is picking up nicely and with a World Cup coming up there are possibilities there.

I would just like to see everybody at the club pulling together. No club is better coached and trained, and no club is better organised. A lot of clubs are in real financial trouble. Not all have been as lucky as Newbury, who have good facilities, or Hungerford, who are keeping on top of the situation. Most are mortgaged up to the hilt.

The club will only get better, and I think they will go on to promotion this season and I just hope the experienced players give the youngsters the benefit of their experience."

Manager Jimmy Kelman joined Hungerford as coach in 1976, succeeding to the manager's chair the following year in one of the club's most important moves. He said "Somebody with his enthusiasm is always a great asset. When Tony came here he carried people along with him, and he has given everybody at the club, including the players some great times. But individuals come and go, and the club has to go on, but Tony will certainly be missed at the club, although he will not be severing his connections entirely."

Mr Williams will remain as a Vice-President and Life 'member of the club; and, just to make the point, on Tuesday he was at Buckingham casting a helpful eye over Hungerford's opponents in the Berks and Bucks Senior Cup.

From an article in the Newbury Weekly News January 1982

Hungerford Town in the Seventies

1. Another Norman Matthews; skipper, centre forward or centre half and an inspiration to the club as player, manager, secretary and the driving force behind the club's general development

2. Local lad, Sid Webb, scoring one of his many goals for Hungerford

3. FA Secretary Ted Croker is introduced to some of Hungerford Town's administrative team, who looked after the clubhouse and ground so efficiently. Pete North introduces Bob Ponsford.

4. Another goal for Ian Farr, Hungerford Town's greatest ever goalscoree

1977 - 1986

After discussing football publications throughout 'The Seventies' with Alan Smith, Chairman of the publishers Queen Anne Press, we had come to the conclusion that Non-League football deserved and would be able to support, an annual publication of its own.

This level of the game had enjoyed a number of monthly magazines, including Greg Tesser's Amateur Footballer and our efforts at Jimmy Hill's Football Weekly, but the title that had become very popular during 'The Seventies' was 'Netstretcher' edited by Jim Voiels and Barry Lenton (of Marine fame) - but there were no annuals.

I enjoyed working closely with Ted Croker, and as I had been producing the FA XI programmes for him, I had been invited to be a co-opted member of the FA Representative Committee and I knew the popular Secretary of The Football Association was in favour of a Non-League book. He was a real football person, an ex-player himself, with Football League experience and a wide knowledge of the Non-League game, a level which included 95% of all football in the country. It was undoubtedly the national sport and was generally attracting a good following.

It was decided we should start with a pocket book size publication, but it was pleasing to be labelled a 'Playfair Annual' as the well established publishers had a good reputation.

With Rothmans retiring from Sports Sponsorship, I had appreciated their offer of a marketing position with them, but had decided to become independent and launched 'Tony Williams (Football Promotions) Ltd. on 1st August 1977. I was lucky to have some good friends at the tobacco company who gave me encouragement and support as I started out on my own.

The football world had taken note of the sponsorship successes introduced by Rothmans for The Northern League, based around Newcastle, and the Isthmian League from the home counties. These two competitions were two of the country's most respected amateur leagues and of course The Western and Hellenic Leagues were also members of the 'Rothmans Family'

All football leagues had now been made fully aware of the advantages of sponsorship and it wasn't long before the huge Non-League world was boosted by support from local companies who were linking their names with the competitions that featured all the major town clubs in their districts.

Adrian Titcombe was one of the hardest working, most dedicated administrators at The Football Association. As competitions Secretary, he was also dedicated to improving the structure of Non-League Football and the reintroduction of an official and respected England side to represent the massive ninety-five percent of the game outside The Football League.

His work on the FA Trophy and the new competition, the FA Vase, was instrumental in both being accepted so successfully, but how could the new England team be introduced? What should it be called, who would be eligible to play in it and who would they play? Help would come from Ted Croker, The Football Association Secretary, who was keen to launch a new England side and had strong Non-League connections.

My involvement with Rothmans had been hugely enjoyable and Adrian had helped the sponsorship all he could from the FA. I knew he had realised the Non-League game deserved a representative team at the highest level, but how would the best semi-professional players be spotted from all over the country?

In fact a caring sponsor was to help The FA in their effort to launch an England Semi-Professional XI. Some years earlier I had played for Dulwich Hamlet for a short spell and had been impressed with the enthusiasm that The Goodliffe Family had for their club and for the game in general. I had also worked for their 'Office Cleaning Services' as a cleaning co-ordinator in the West End, so knew OCS was a positive and well run company. Perhaps they might like to help the new manager Howard Wilkinson and the FA, develop a new 'England' team at the level with which they had been involved for many years.

Ted Croker and Adrian Titcombe obviously sold the idea successfully and the O.C.S. Inter-League Cup was launched with four leagues represented in the 1978-1979 season. The Isthmian (Manager: Brian Lee), Northern League (Manager Stan Bradley), Southern League (Manager: Barry Watling) and Northern Premier (Manager: Bob Murphy).

My company obviously had experience with the Rothmans sponsorship ideals and could help others if needed. Our little Non-League Football Annual had been launched for the 1978-1979 season and of course featured the previous 1977-1978 campaign, remembered for Blyth Spartans amazing FA Cup run which actually took them into the draw for The Sixth Round of The FA Challenge Cup - a Non-League club was in the quarter final draw!

Spartans were a wonderful advert for the Non-League game and coming from one of the Rothmans leagues, possible new sponsors were alerted all over the country. Plans for a supreme national Non-League competition were being discussed and there was massive respect for clubs like Altrincham, Bath City, Boston United, Enfield, Scarborough, Telford United, Weymouth, Wigan Athletic, Wycombe Wanderers and Yeovil Town. All these clubs were well supported, and given the opportunity, would surely hold their own in the Football League.

The Non-League world and indeed, the three national Football Association Knock Out competitions, The FA Cup, FA Trophy and FA Vase, would benefit from extra publicity and hopefully our publications might be able to help.

We had also enjoyed promoting the Office Cleaning Services sponsorship of an Inter League knock out competition for their representative teams. These games provided the ideal trial games

1977 - 1986

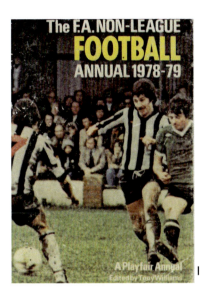

1. First FA Non-League Football Annual
2. FA XI v SW Co 77
3. Inter League Cup 1979
4. With Adrian Titcombe, handing over an award to Enfield Manager Eddie McCluskie
5. A much appreciated present from the Daily Express cartoonist Roy Ullyett

1977 - 1986

for Howard Wilkinson, the manager of the new England Semi-Professional International squad, who won the initial knock out tournament contested by Scotland, Italy and Holland at the end of the 1978-1979 season.

Non-League football was getting more glamorous and we had the means to promote all the exciting developments by helping with match day programmes and, of course, giving full coverage in Non-League football's own little annual.

Publicity for the 1979 FA Trophy and FA Vase competitions had shown an improvement. Attendances at Wembley, being an encouraging 32,000 for Stafford Rangers v Kettering Town, plus 17,500 for Billericay Town v Almondsbury Greenway.

Our second annual welcomed the introduction of The Alliance Premier League for the 1979-1980 season, a competition introduced to give the cream of Non-League football the chance to prove they were the best outside The Football League and worthy of a chance to join the Fourth Division.

Great work by Adrian Titcombe of the Football Association and the senior officials from The Southern and Northern Premier Leagues worked tirelessly to set up a well structured pyramid of leagues, giving the chance to any ambitious club to progress right up into The Football League.

Having worked closely with The Football Association regarding FA XI programmes and The FA Cup Reviews I also became involved in plans for Chairman Sir Harold Thompson and Secretary Ted Croker to produce an FA Magazine!

The two top men really found it difficult to get on happily together. They were from completely different backgrounds and looked at the game from very different perspectives. I agreed to edit their new idea (but whose idea was it?). 'FA To-day' was launched in October 1979 and potentially it really should have been an excellent replacement for the old FA News which was apparently considered out of date.

Right from the beginning, my role as editor was a 'deathtrap' as the Chairman thought I was 'his man' and Ted Croker thought the magazine really wasn't The Chairman's responsibility. The potential was massive but I was relieved when the battling came to an end after two years.

With England Semi-Pros now competing in a regular end of season Four Nations Tournament, the Non-League world was enjoying an exciting period. We were pleased to be involved, and after our three early pocket book editions, the 1981-1982 season saw the annual develop into 'The Rothmans FA Non-League Football Yearbook' an A5 size, sponsored publication.

This was particularly pleasing for me after my bitter sweet memories of the Rothmans Football Yearbook. It was good to know the special company, where I had enjoyed the sponsorship work so much, were prepared to back my ideas and for the next three years, Non-League football once again had a publication that attempted to promote their levels of the national game.

I had been working with Geoff Peters of the Publishers Queen Anne Press and Brian Roach at Rothmans, with Ted Croker, Adrian Titcombe and Steve Clark giving great support and encouragement from The Football Association. Thanks to Geoff Peters enthusiasm we had helped Rothmans develop an impressive collection of sponsored Yearbooks and our third Rothmans Non-League Yearbook contained a record 512 pages.

The publishers offered me a chance to return as Editor of The Rothmans Football Yearbook that I had introduced fourteen years previously. I enjoyed the years work with Geoff Peters, the publication and of course Rothmans, but a troubled political publishing situation did effect the happy working relationship. Sadly, the Rothmans involvement lost momentum and a previously happy team broke up.

It had all been extremely enjoyable when the yearbooks were developed. I remember visiting Wigan Rugby League Club and seeing a very young teenage prospect called Andy Farrell being shown around by the officials of Rugby League's top club, who were also interested in our idea of Rugby League and Rugby Union Yearbooks.

Having decided to work away from the security of Rothmans in the mid eighties, it was very difficult although challenging and satisfying, but not conducive to happy and steady responsibilities of marriage.

It was extremely difficult for Hilary to accept my way of life, in which I must have appeared to be putting work (which all centered around football) before normal acceptable family responsibilities. I was not providing my half of a proper married partnership and I quite understood (although badly shaken) when Hilary decided to return to Devon.

The thought of losing contact with the children was sickening and trying to sort out life without the family and a proper home didn't make the work any easier. New, but very testing challenges that I actually enjoyed, were looking after my three children for three half term weeks, a week in the Easter and Christmas school holidays plus two weeks in the Summer holidays.

Hilary had met Phil, an extremely genuine, decent, single neighbour in South Devon and was of course pleased to have those weeks free to get to know him without having to look after the children.

The fact that I had three youngsters for seven weeks of the year gave me plenty of experience with Michael, Katy and John Probably more than I would have had as a married Dad working long hours. I would have always been playing catch up with them after leaving early in the morning and returning late, plus my involvement with football on Saturdays.

As it was, we had a lot of fun going to shows, zoos, staying at hotels in which I had friends in management and of course going

1977 - 1986

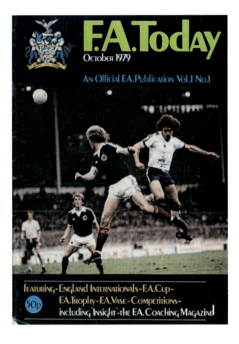
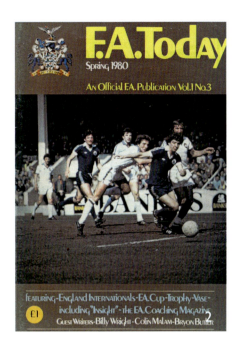
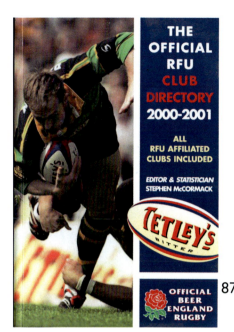

No.	Club	P	W	D	L	F	A	Pts
1	Altrincham	38	24	8	6	79	35	56
2	Weymouth	38	22	10	6	73	37	54
3	Worcester City	38	19	11	8	53	36	49
4	Boston United	38	16	13	9	52	43	45
5	Gravesend & Northfleet	38	17	10	11	49	44	44
6	Maidstone United	38	16	11	11	54	37	43
7	Kettering Town	38	15	13	10	55	50	43
8	Northwich Victoria	38	16	10	12	50	38	42
9	Bangor City	38	14	14	10	41	46	42
10	Nuneaton Borough	38	13	13	12	58	44	39
11	Scarborough	38	12	15	11	47	38	39
12	Yeovil Town	38	13	10	15	46	49	36
13	Telford United	38	13	8	17	52	60	34
14	Barrow	38	14	6	18	47	55	34
15	Wealdstone	38	9	15	14	42	54	33
16	Bath City	38	10	12	16	43	69	32
17	Barnet	38	10	10	18	32	48	30
18	A.P. Leamington	38	7	11	20	32	63	25
19	Stafford Rangers	38	6	10	22	41	57	22
20	Redditch United	38	5	8	25	26	69	18

1. F.A. To-Day Vol 1 No 1

2. F.A. To-Day Spring 80

3. Rugby

4. The final league table for the first year of the Football Conference in 1979-1980

1977 - 1986

to football matches. We got to to know each other a lot better than we would in a normal married household. I think that bond has remained throughout life and without anyone losing any of the respect and love for Hilary, a wonderful mother.

My social life had developed from the state of feeling a complete failure, as a divorced man, until I realised a large percentage of people I was meeting were also divorced. So I enjoyed a very exciting social life, in a very different world to the one I had originally known as a young bachelor.

I took advantage of my freedom to listen to my jazz favourites, Kenny Ball, Acker Bilk and Chris Barber plus Tommy Burton, a particularly lively jazz pianist and the new boys on the block, Chas & Dave. Tim Hale, a local friend who had also suffered a recent divorce agreed to run The Newbury Jazz club with me and life became very full and great fun. My Hungerford Town football connection was still important, and touring the country watching football at all levels was fulfilling but tiring, although our books were proving popular and very satisfying.

I thoroughly enjoyed SAGA trips abroad for singles and on the very last day of a holiday in the West Indies I met a charming American lady Diane Lavois and we promised to keep in touch. I learnt through our letters, that Diane was battling against Multiple Sclerosis and had to take on all sorts of jobs to raise enough money to pay her medical bills. Diane was remarkably cheerful for someone with such bad luck.

Our new style Yearbook proved very popular and being involved with a football promotions company I enjoyed the work which included sponsorship, fundraising advertising and general promotions.

I had met John Watt at a few Football Writers social engagements and he had helped with a Rothmans book promotion in Manchester when he had introduced me to the newly appointed manager Alex Ferguson, who explained he was having a difficult time settling with United, as results hadn't been great!

John was an experienced sporting Scotsman who had great contacts in football and he suggested I might like to help him with the job of hosting matchday guests for Queens Park Rangers at Shepherd's Bush.

What a lovely job, meeting sponsors, the press and assorted football personalities! The only problem was watching the football at their 'Omniturf pitch', the club's very severe and difficult surface that was nothing like normal grass. We also enjoyed working with the supporters club for whom we organised some Football Quizzes and the social life was enjoyable at a very happy club where the directors, players and staff seemed to mix very well.

It was a very pleasant surprise when Newnes Books decided to publish a League Club Directory and asked me to build a suitable editorial team. The well established publishers would now be presenting a full coverage of British football in 1985, through a new 'League Club Directory' and the established Non-League Club Directory.

Our editorial team included experienced and very helpful publisher Tony Bagley and his colleague Chris Pow from Newnes. Peter Arnold the House Editor, ensured the facts were presented in a neat and readable fashion and Tony Pullein and Barry Hugman brought great experience as well known football statisticians. Each club also had a statistician nominated by Ray Spiller the organiser of 'The Association of The Football Statisticians' to help us if needed and sports fanatic Bill Mitchell was a much appreciated assistant editor.

Just six weeks before the publication of the 1986 edition of the League Club Directory, the driving force behind the Newnes Books sports publications Tony Bagley died. His encouragement and support had been greatly appreciated and hopefully our Football Directories will always act as a special memorial to his hard work and friendship.

I was about to experience a complete change in lifestyle as a phone call from old friend Tony Brown, the ex Gloucestershire Cricket captain, had suggested I applied for the position as marketing executive at The Somerset County Cricket club, where he was now the County Secretary. But what about the publishing? The Non-League book was in its tenth year and hard work was needed to establish The League Club Directory.

Newnes Books without Tony Bagley was just not the same, and it wasn't long before I heard that the company would not be publishing the two Football Directories. So I had responsibility for two excellent books that had proved popular and which we were proud to have compiled. It didn't take long to decide that we should publish the books ourselves or rather I would have to publish the books myself!

The launch for our first two Directories at the beginning of the 1986-1987 season was held at the Football Association Headquarters at Lancaster Gate. This was a privilege, but it was also very pleasing to be presented with a plaque subscribed :-

*'To Tony Williams, for his continual promotion
of all that is good in football'.*

Meanwhile Michael was playing rugby and sprinting well at Kingsbridge School in Devon, although he also appeared to be developing a natural love of football. Katy was also sprinting well and growing up fast into a lovely young lady and John was showing great skills on the football pitch, but his team played in Kingsbridge, South Devon on Sundays which meant a busy weekend. There were more and more of their achievements I wished I could see but I was too far away.

1977 - 1986

1. Eight popular jazz bands would entertain on two Jazz Boats going from London Bridge to Southend and back on a Sunday. The bands would swap boats in Essex. and return up the Thames in London with the bands and their fans enjoying a warm evening after a days drinking - A very good time was had by all.

3. 'The Fabulous Three' Katy, Michael and John through the ages

2. Diane Lavois - over the years we have kept in touch by telephone and christmas cards and have both visited each other's country. Diane is seen here at the football bar in my home/office in Helland, a part of North Curry.

4. Maurice Evans an old friend from Reading Football Club had kindly driven down to present the end of season awards at The Kingsbridge Boys Awards evening and is seen here with John who had enjoyed a great season.

1986 - 1991

When the children came up to stay with me, Mike would sometimes look after the others on the train to Reading, but on this occasion I arranged to meet them at Taunton station, as we were to drive over to see my sister Caroline who lived in Yeovil.

On the way we passed through Hatch Beauchamp and the children spotted Tim Hale, our old friend from Yattendon days, who was renovating a cottage with a view to selling it on when the job was finished.

I was due to attend an interview at Somerset Cricket Club, apparently there were a number of applicants for the Marketing position, but the interview seemed to go quite well and as I knew county secretary Tony Brown I thought I must have a good chance to get the job.

The phone call came quite quickly from the chairman, I had come a close second, 'but thank you very much you just missed out!' Disappointing, but perhaps I should just concentrate on my football interests. However, one day later there was another call from Taunton. The chosen one had turned down the County's offer and Tony Brown had pointed out that as I had been told I was the runner-up, presumably I should be offered the position.

The timing was perfect, as I was able to afford Tim Hale's cottage and he was able to finish it around me. I would be living very close to The County Ground at Taunton and I could work on my annual football books from the cottage in the evenings.

Somerset County Cricket Club had a glamorous reputation with Ian Botham, Viv Richards and Joel Garner world famous cricketing characters. Unfortunately I didn't have much pre-season time to sell enough advertising or sign up match day sponsors. Ideally a marketing executive really needed a couple of seasons to develop contacts, but I did introduce match day programmes to include scorecards!

One very different attitude that I found within senior cricket, compared with football, was the massive barrier between those being paid by the club and the volunteer amateurs who were treated in a completely different way. The old Gentleman v Players situation still lingered, but amazingly it was noticeable off the field as well as in the dressing room.

The junior professionals really weren't paid enough to see them comfortably through the winter months and sometimes we saw well known county players taking holiday jobs such as Christmas postmen.

I thoroughly enjoyed my involvement with the very friendly and talented squad of players but my contribution to the club was very limited. I organised some fund raising football matches which Viv and Ian seemed to really enjoy, in fact they both signed forms at Hungerford Town after a charity game that also benefitted from Joel Garner serving behind the bar! Not surprisingly, the boys never had the chance to play for their new club.

Tony Brown was sometimes asked to sort out 'social misunderstandings' that the two stars had got into during their evening 'trips' around the county. I felt very honoured that I was allowed in the changing room and it was listening to the banter that I realised the competitive spirit that existed between Ian and Viv, the two great friends. The rest of the players understood the situation and everyone benefitted from the two players always giving their very best, but their outstanding fame did make them public targets when the cider flowed!

Club captain Peter Roebuck was a very different type of cricketer to the county's stars and it was quite obvious that he had great difficulty keeping the dressing room positive and happy. Somerset had the glamour and the stars who could entertain the fans better than any other county, but those close to the team knew there was always the chance of an 'explosion'. Vic Marks had the personality and the talent to be accepted by all the varying characters in the dressing room, and Secretary Tony Brown the senior full time administrator, benefited from all his experience collected from his career with Gloucestershire and his managerial roles with MCC.

Ian Botham was very popular, and was friendly and helpful, but his much larger than life personality and love of a party could be uncontrollable, while Viv was also very friendly and polite but sometimes moody. Both were very kind and helpful to me and it was always exciting to see them in action. When I was introducing my son Michael to Viv, the great man said 'hello Michael my name's Viv' and Mike couldn't get over the fact that he was so humble for such a famous sportsman.

I enjoyed the 1986 season with the county. I felt it was an honour to work with such quality sportsmen for a quality club. My chairman Michael Hill was a kind and friendly man who loved his cricket, but what really made me realise I was in the wrong job was the fact that, as the *Professional* Marketing Executive, I was not welcome at the meetings of The County's *Amateur* Marketing Committee, made up of farmers, businessmen and retired executives all obviously unpaid. The cricketing world was indeed living in the past.

I had enjoyed my year and learnt a lot about our famous summer sport. It was good to work with my old friend Tony Brown, but one memory that we always smile about was when Tony had phoned me at the club to say he had been delayed and could I pick up his wife's father who would be waiting outside the hospital after his check up.

I duly drove round, picked up the gentleman and returned to Tony, who was then back in his office, but found I had picked up the wrong old man - who was suitably confused at being kidnapped!

I thoroughly enjoy returning to watch cricket at the Taunton county ground, Michael Hill is still enjoying the club and I also keep in touch with Tony Brown who has returned to Bristol

1986 - 1991

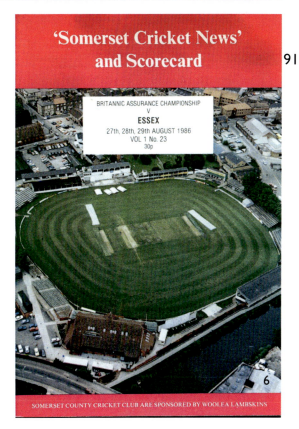

1. Hatch Beauchamp Cottage
2. Helland Home and Office, North Curry
3. Somerset Cricket Team 1986
4. Tony Brown, Somerset Cricket Club Secretary
5. Michael Hill, Somerset Cricket Club Secretary
6. Somerset v Essex August 1986

1986 - 1991

where he enjoyed such a great career with Gloucestershire.

I had continued to work on our football publications as the two Directories were now my responsibility and we decided to publish them ourselves as sales had been reasonable. The Football Association were helping as usual with Adrian Titcombe and Steve Clark on the editorial panel. Contributors volunteered help from all over the country and we had production aid from Orchard Typesetting in Weston-super-Mare and Sovereign Print Works in Sidmouth.

To attend a full variety of matches I obviously had to travel further on a Saturday and I also spent most Sundays driving down to Kingsbridge in South Devon, where I helped coach John's Kingsbridge Youth side and realised that my youngest was a very exciting prospect indeed!

The Summer of 1988 produced some very pleasant surprises. I had become good friends with Lew Clark, an ex Police Officer who had retired. We met when he was looking after the stewards at The Somerset County Ground and had enjoyed some happy social evenings with his wife Nina and his family, in his very pleasant house in Helland just outside North Curry.

Lew and Nina were hoping to move into a new home which had been built on their land so were planning to sell their old home. I fancied a move into a bigger building where we could develop an official working area and asked Lew if I could have first refusal. He was planning a holiday, but although he didn't think I could find the asking price, he agreed to give me the first option when they returned in a couple of weeks time.

The very next week we heard that The Daily Mail wanted

> Well, this is where one thinks there must be some extra terrestrial power looking after you. It really was a wonderful year!

to buy The League Club Directory for a price that would enable me to buy Helland Cottage, having sold my Hatch Beauchamp home. My excited Bank Manager actually wanted to hold the cheque when it arrived and obviously the sadness and financial wreckage of the divorce could now be shaken off. Tony Williams Publications could spread its wings a little in the new facility and perhaps we could produce some more titles from our new home.

Michael was now working with us and George Brown, a dour Scotsman who lived locally, was an extremely hard worker and a very reliable colleague. We were helped with Secretarial work by Domini Fevin and my old friends Peter & Colleen Grove, who also enjoyed writing and publishing, were always keen to help if needed.

Looking back at The Barclays League Football Club Directory, which was launched in 1985, it is interesting to note the emphasis we put on our 'Good News Awards'. Even then the constant criticism of the game in the media had inspired us to try and redress the balance and publicise the national game's good news, that was also constantly available for all to see and enjoy.

I was excited to have been invited to act as Press Officer for England's Semi-Professionals tour to Italy 1988-1989. James Wright also joined us and we included a full report in our magazines. The other good news that season was the obvious enthusiasm being shown in the Daily Mail sports offices. Sally Cartwright led a lively and very positive team of publishers who had suggested we should compile a Non-League monthly magazine to be produced as a Daily Mail publication with an editorial office in North Curry!

Attendances were increasing throughout the Non-League competitions, with The FA Trophy and FA Vase proving very popular. So 1989-90 seemed a perfect time to introduce a new magazine to further promote the levels of the game that involved such a huge percentage of the country's football enthusiasts.

A very happy working relationship was developed and a match was played at the Kingstonian ground between The Mail and The Non-League Club Directory with a celebrity kick-off by Sally. It was particularly special to me as it was one of the first occasions I had seen my two sons Michael and John playing in an adult game together.

I had thoroughly enjoyed helping with coaching Kingsbridge boys Sunday league side and it was good to hear that John was selected to play for South Devon Under 14s as he had enjoyed a very successful free scoring season. Driving from Taunton to Kingsbridge every Sunday wasn't always fun, especially returning soaked, but not having been available to take him to week day training and matches after school, I was pleased to be able to contribute to my youngest son's development, especially as he seemed to genuinely love the game.

During the 1989-1990 season I had been flattered to have been in a position to help with England Semi-Professional squad's administration. The first game was against Wales at Merthyr in which the home side selected their squad from all over Britain for the first time and achieved a goalless draw.

In mid season, having been invited to travel with the England Semi-Professional side as Honorary Press Officer I had enjoyed the experience greatly, becoming very good friends with manager Tony Jennings.

At the end of the season, with The Football Association staff busy on senior football duties, I was invited to stand in for Adrian Titcombe as England's Admin Tour Manager to Eire alongside Team Manager Tony Jennings. I considered

1986 - 1991

Schoolboy football in the cities is well organised and very competitive. But in some more rural areas hardly any games are played and it relies on the enthusiasm of individual schoolteachers to organise the selection and preparation of regional squads. In the South West an Under 14 competition was contested by ten regions with Torbay and Plymouth eliminating Exeter, East Cornwall and West Cornwall while Bristol and Taunton put out North Devon, Bridgwater and Yeovil. The semi finals saw Torbay beat Taunton 11-0 and Plymouth beat Bristol 3-1. In the final the side from little Torbay who improved with every game under the guidence of John Ashton and helpers won convincingly against the powerful favourites from Plymouth despite losing three key players. Slomka, White and Williams scored in an excellent 3-1 victory which was only the fourth the area had recorded in sixty years.

1. North Curry Office
2. John with Devon's Under 14 South West representative team
3. John
4. Michael
5. John & Mike at Kingstonian

1986 - 1991

this a great honour but I was really thrilled when Chris Wilcox, Chairman of the Committee, presented me with my England International tie, which has been treasured ever since.

The end of the season was disappointing when Hungerford Town lost badly at Sudbury in the second leg of the FA Vase Semi-Final, (this was the third time they had lost just one step from Wembley). However a holiday in St Lucia was a great success and on the very last evening, I met Diane Lavois (who I mentioned earlier) a charming American lady and we promised to keep in touch, which we have done for 25 years.

Social life at home was boosted by membership of 'Solos' a singles club which was great fun. At the end of the season I watched The Old Malvernians beat The Old Brentwood 3-1 to win the Arthur Dunn Cup. Little did we know it would be over 25 years before they could do it again.

Another memorable Saturday was enjoyed at the South Western League End of Season Awards dinner at Liskeard. During the evening, reports on the vital Division One game between Arsenal and Liverpool was filtering through.

Arsenal had to win by two goals and with injury time being played The Gunners were still just leading 1-0. As that excellent film 'Fever Pitch' highlighted brilliantly, Arsenal won with a second goal in the last seconds and won The Championship. As a Liverpool supporter since my friendship with Roger Hunt, I was disappointed, but many Arsenal supporters will treasure that evening for the rest of their lives.

Italian Tour 1988 - 1989

THE ITALIAN JOB

YOU will all get an early morning call – at 5 o'clock!

Yes, it is an honour to be selected for England and there's no doubt that a trip to the continent is exciting but the players certainly earn their 'caps' when they represent The England Semi-Professional side.

On Saturday 25th February the England squad travelled from all over England to meet at The Crest Hotel, Gatwick where manager Tony Jennings, F.A. Executive Adrian Titcombe and Doctor Alan Tabor sorted out a fit squad to travel to Italy for a friendly game at Salerno. Of the original selection, Phil Gridelet (Barnet), Steve Brooks (Cheltenham Town) and Steve Hanlon (Macclesfield Town) were pulled out by their clubs, having received knocks during the afternoon.

A number of players were on stand by and in this case the lucky ones to get the call were: Mark Hone (Welling United) with Andy Hessenthaler and Steve Conner (both Dartford). I was at Yeovil Town watching their F.A. Trophy tie with Barrow and having been thrilled with the request from the F.A. to travel as the Public Relations and Press Officer I was able to give Glenn Skivington, the Barrow defender, a lift to join the England team for his first match. Sadly his colleague Kenny Lowe, who was also on standby, didn't make it this time but hopefully his day will come.

The trip to Sussex seemed to fly by as Glenn and I talked football

'Doc' Tabor and Tony Jennings strap on a 'new foot' to enable Paul Furlong win his first cap.   Photo: Adrian Titcombe

nonstop. It was interesting to hear of his times at Derby County and Southend United and after our chat I can see why Barrow have created such a good impression in the Conference this season and have cultivated such a fine club spirit. Glenn who is studying for a law degree has the utmost respect for their manager, Ray Wilkie and the team of officials who work so hard in awkward conditions up there in their North West outpost.

We were amongst the first to arrive at the hotel but the lads gradually turned up from their Conference, Trophy and Beazer Homes games. It was a spectacular sight to see all the very colourful tracksuits that clubs now use for the players as casual gear and top marks went to Enfield for design and colour, although this did nothing to make up for the depressing result they had suffered in the afternoon!

Tony Jennings called a meeting to introduce the newcomers and ensure everyone knew the plans for the next day. He was thrilled with the fact so many of his original squad were fit and available and that the reserves were all from the original standby nominations. We had come over the first hurdle reasonably well.

So it was off to bed with the thought that those bells would be calling us at 5 o'clock am!

The squad who all managed to get to the airport on time, looking smart and just about awake were rewarded by a flight that left on time and presented us with a very reasonable breakfast. I thoroughly enjoyed a chat with Antone Joseph, England's most capped player on the trip, who had just moved to Kidderminster Harriers. Having had a tremendous Trophy record at Telford he was hoping that he could be off to Wembley again with The Harriers. I was particularly impressed that Antone had bought every one of the Non-League Football magazines – he deserves to get to Wembley!

The journey from Naples to Salerno is not one of the most picturesque in Italy and I'm sure that Italians wouldn't want their country judged by this trip. However, on arriving at the excellent 'Jolly Hotel' we were entertained to an enjoyable lunch and the players were able to get their heads down and rest before planning the evening's 'operation'.

At this time of year in Italy all the little children are dressed up in colourful fancy dress and the whole town seemed to be involved in a carnival. The traffic was solid throughout the area and everyone seemed amazingly relaxed as families strolled around the town.

A squad of tracksuited Italians were also in the hotel and they looked massive. Keeping the ball on the ground seemed to be our order of the night – but they turned out to be a volley ball team!

The Solerno club were in the 'C' Division of the Italian League, who have divisions 'A' and 'B' as full-time professionals with three regional 'C' divisions of part-time professionals. The teams most likely to gain promotion tend to have a number of full-time players in readiness for 'B' division football and Solerno were near the top of their league. However

Now the players have gone, where's the tea? Tony Jennings and Ron Reid have just finished their pre-match talk.   Photo: Adrian Titcombe

95

Italian Tour 1988 - 1989

Continued from previous article

there were no local boys in the Italian Team which was selected from the 'C' Divisions and were under-21.

Three thousand fans arrived to watch an impressive display of marching and band music before the game when the players emerged from hole win the ground (more impressive than just running out of a tunnel) the England team was (4-4-2): John McKenna & Paul Shirtliff both (Boston United), Dave Howell (Enfield), Glenn Skivington (Barrow), Paul Watts (Redbridge Forest), Andy Hessenthaler (Dartford), Paul Rogers (Sutton United), Antone Joseph (Kidderminster Harriers), Gary Simpson (Altrincham), Paul Furlong (Enfield) and Mark Carter (Runcorn). Not surprisingly the Itlalians looked the livelier side in the first-half and McKenna did well to keep them out with two good saves in the first 30 minutes. England were steady, with Skivington, Howell and Rogers looking sound at the heart of the defense but it was a cross from the dangerous Italian right-winger that set up a neat near post headed goal for Favi.

We hadn't really settled down but after the interval, with a much livelier attitude England dominated proceedings without ever looking really dangerous. Gary Simpson had superb half and Paul Furlong and Mark Carter worked hard at the front. Andy Papa, Mark Hone, Steve Conner, Paul Bancroft and Robbie Cook all got into the action for McKenna (45 mins), Shirtliff (60 mins), Hessenthaler (45 mins), Watts (45 mins) and Paul Rogers (77mins) respectively.

Despite playing well in the second period a second goal was unluckily conceded when the Italian's broke away and Favor's nudge over the line was allowed despite a little flutter of the linesman's flag. Perhaps 2-0 was a fair result but certainly it was a worthwhile exercise, all the new caps acquitted themselves well and a lot of experience gained by all.

In the evening the lads enjoyed a quiet drink but were a little worried by the sight of a number of Italian men dancing to themselves in the mirror and decided this wasn't a case for 'when in Rome' etc (or Salerno) and returned to the hotel for an early night. Meanwhile the officials attended a 'banquet' that started at midnight and ended at about 3.00a.m .Unfortunately the Chairman of the representatives committee Chris Wilcox was unwell so second in command Jack Barter made the speeches and it was a very tired party that eventually got bed, having been up for over 20 hours!

After a restful morning and another excellent lunch the whole party visited the famous ruins at Pompei before taking the coach back to the airport and a return to Gatwick at about 9.00p.m.

It had been a very tiring but extremely enjoyable tow days. Saturday evening seemed weeks ago and an excellent spirit had developed within the party while the attitude often players both on an doff the field had been exemplary. the build up to the game had really given them very little chance of success but they had all obviously been proud to represent their country and the management team of Tony Jennings and Ron Reid were most certainly proud of their efforts.

As usual the Italian Football Association had been perfect hosts and our constant guide Dario Bianchi and the organisation of 'C' Division secretary Marinella Conigliaro was once again a great help to us all. In just one weeks time it would be off to Lillishall for preparation for the game at Merthyr Tydfil against the Welsh and there was no doubt that the experience and spirit gained in Italy would be appreciated.

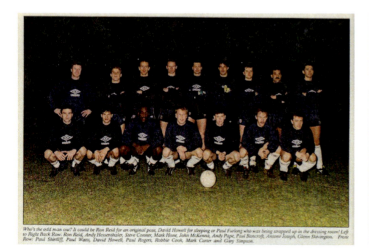

Who's the odd man out? It could be Ron Reid for an original pose, David Howell for sleeping or Paul Furlong who was being strapped up in the dressing room! Left to Right Back Row: Ron Reid, Andy Hessenthaler, Steve Conner, Mark Hone, John McKenna, Andy Pape, Paul Bancroft, Antone Joseph, Glenn Skivington. Front Row: Paul Shirtliff, Paul Watts, David Howell, Paul Rogers, Robbie Cook, Mark Carter and Gary Simpson.

'Up Pompei' A smart England party rest amongst the ruins.   Photo: T.W.

Italian Tour 1988 - 1989

The England playing squad on the best area of grass at Turners Cross | **Back Row L-R:** Andy Pape, Glenn Skivington, Paul Rogers, Paul Bancroft, David Howell, Paul Furlong, Noel Ashford, Phil Gridelet, Mark Carter and John McKenna. **Front Row:** Paul Watts, Gary Simpson, Antone Joseph, Paul Shirtliff, Andrew Clarke and Steve Brooks. Photo: T.W.

ENGLAND SUCCESS STORY

It's all very well going on a football trip when you can sidle off to the bar at every available free moment and leave 'them' to organise travel arrangements, coach times, hotel rooms, meal arrangements and co-operation with the press, our supporters who have travelled to the games, the travelling council members and the 'home' F.A. officials.

I had enjoyed that role immensely and took it for granted that everything just went smoothly automatically. Well, Adrian Titcombe the Football Association administrator who had looked after every previous England Semi-Professional squad was in Italy and I had certainly considered it an honour to be asked to help out in his absence.

As it turned out 'the team' of Manager Tony Jennings, with assistance from Ron Reid plus Doctor Tim Sonnex (Arsenal), Physio Dave Butler (Spurs) and two experienced Council members in the Chairman of the Representative Committee, Chris Wilcox and Bill Wilson carried me along well and I thoroughly enjoyed the experience!

No England International side had beaten a Southern Ireland team for a very long time and sadly the playing surfaces at Dalymont Park, Dublin (home of Bohemians) and then Turners Cross (home of Cork City) were really very depressing and I could imagine it would be very hard to persuade players to give 'their all' on such dangerous pitches.

So full marks to 'Jenno' for turning out two squads who didn't shirk a single tackle and matched two very spirited Irish sides in every facet of the game. The fact that we were better organised as a team and were also individually more skillful were only to be proved once the physical battles had been won.

In the first match, with Andrew 'Terrorhawk' Clarke making his debut after a great season with Barnet, the Irish took the lead with a good shot by Stephen O'Reilly following a well worked free kick after fifteen minutes. But ace England goalscorer Mark Carter accepted a pass from one of the tour's great successes, Gary Simpson and equalised ten minutes after half time. He then scored the winner from the penalty spot having been tripped himself and England might well have increased the lead in the remaining thirteen minutes.

So the bubble had been broken - an England team had beaten Eire. Would this be a good omen for the full England squad preparing for a meeting with Jack Charlton's boys in a few days time? The whole of Ireland was captivated by the World Cup and while we were there poor Bobby Robson had to suffer another vitriolic and quite unfair attack from the tabloid press. Everyone on the trip felt sick for him but I noticed that when buying papers for the long railway trips to and from Cork many of our lads still bought those papers. Considering none of them cover semi-professional football (while most of the more respected papers give excellent coverage) this was sad. If everyone who really felt upset by the unkind, unfair and often untrue stories that shatter so many peoples lives, just bought other papers then perhaps the message might just get through and the quality of sports journalism might improve.

So, with one win under our belt it was a very happy party that moved on to Cork. One of the highlights of our stay in Dublin was the constant 'protection' and guidance of our motor cycle escorts. These two policeman put the fear of god into all in our way as we sped through a busy city with a feeling of great importance. It was greatly appreciated lads - thanks very much! (they asked for a mention in the magazine and they have even got photographic coverage as well!).

The Turners Cross pitch was a nightmare and as the game was played in the afternoon sun it had all the omens of a disaster. However, England never allowed the home side to settle and an early first International goal by Paul Furlong probably impressed the watching Chairman and Chief Scout of Birmingham City. England were two up after fifteen minutes when Noel Ashford rose to power in a perfect header and move him clear into second place in England's goalscorers.

However, Mark Carter scored his third of the tour to give him twelve goals in ten games and England ran out comfortable and impressive winners. John 'Tacklebury' McKenna certainly didn't let down the scouse reputation for 'ready wit' and the 'experience' of 'senior pro' Ashford was noticed along with the 'pulling power' of Gary Simpson when it came to very young fans in the hotel.

The whole squad had once again proved to be superb ambassadors for their sport, their clubs and their country. Dave Howell's captaincy on and off the field was an inspiration and fine support to the whole party while all playing reputations were upheld although now Glenn Skivington, the successful Trophy winning captain from Barrow had difficulty shaking off a bruised thigh.

It was a privilege to be with this tour and for those loyal supporters from Enfield, Hyde United, Altincham, Stafford Rangers and the United Counties League amongst others, I am sure the week-end will be remembered for a long time with a great deal of pleasure.

> It was a privilege to be one of the party

The England squad with officials before the first International against Eire at Dalymont Park: **Back Row:** Mark Carter, Glenn Skivington, Gary Simpson, Paul Furlong, Phil Gridelet, Tim Sonnex (Doctor), John McKenna, Tony Jennings, Andy Pape, Ron Reid, Dave Butler (Physio) Steve Brooks, Paul Bancroft, and Antone Joseph. **Front Row:** Paul Watts, Paul Shirtliff, David Howell, Bill Wilson (Council Member) Chris Wilcox (Chairman of FA Committee), Noel Ashford, Paul Rogers, Andrew Clarke. Photo: Colin Atkinson

Above:
The other team.
Left to right : John McKenna 'Tacklebury', Dave Butler, Tony Jennings, Tim Sonnex, Andy 'Terror Hawk' Clarke, Paul Bancroft, Steve Brooks, Glenn Skivington.

Wales & Eire Tours 1989 - 1990

The Importance of
The FA Trophy and
FA Vase for Non-League Clubs

by Ted Croker

Secretary of the Football Association

"Non-League Football" is a term that has come to mean the layer of football below the Football League and generally involving clubs with their own self-contained ground. This Directory is long overdue and will I am sure be a very interesting guide and record of a very important level of football.

Non-League football has its two national knock-out competitions, now well established, and its own representative national team. The history of the more senior of the two club competitions, the Challenge Trophy, is scarcely a long one, dating back only to 1969. It was inaugurated to provide competition for professional or semi-professional clubs outside the Football League. These clubs were not, of course, able to enter the Amateur Challenge Cup, and the Challenge Trophy now gave a whole stratum of clubs a realistic chance of an appearance in a Wembley final.

When the status of "amateur" was abolished by the FA Council and the Amateur Cup discontinued as a result in 1974, it heralded a new interest and keenness for the Trophy competition. It became the premier non-League knock-out Cup and now included a hundred or so of the leading clubs who had previously played in the Amateur Cup. A number of these clubs had achieved some measure of fame – for example Barnet, Bishop Auckland, Crook Town and Hendon.

The impact made by these ex-"amateur" teams was not great in the first two years of their participation in the new competition, but the semi-final draw in 1977 which paired Dagenham and Slough Town ensured a first appearance in the Final for a club from the Amateur Cup. The integration was complete in 1980, with Dagenham's victory over Mossley, and then merely emphasised in the following year with Bishop's Stortford and Sutton United providing an all-Isthmian League Final.

It seems unlikely that the attendances at Trophy finals will ever match those huge Amateur Cup final gates, particularly those in the 1950s, and the present record for the Trophy is 32,000 – in 1979. Clearly there is a great deal of public interest in the Trophy competition, although publicity for it in the national newspapers is scarcely extensive, and it is interesting to note that the Final is regularly played before a larger crowd than at something like thirty Football League matches played on the same afternoon. Usually, of course, the size of the Final gate depends on the sort of home attendances that the two competing clubs are regularly able to draw.

Last April saw the Challenge Vase Final contested for the tenth time. The Vase effectively replaced the Amateur Cup in 1974 and – with the most successful Amateur Cup clubs switching to the Trophy – this second new competition provided the remaining clubs with an opportunity to grab the headlines and, of course, to play at Wembley, which they had scarcely had before.

The Vase finalists have comprised a cross-section of clubs – some long established, some recently formed — from many different areas of the country and for many the Vase has been the springboard for further success.

Page from Wales Programme at Merthyr 89-90

Top : The England bench watching the Italian match

Below: Admin' in Eire The 'Back up Squad':
Right to left: Tony Jennings (Team Manager),
Ron Reid
(Assistant Manager), Tony Williams, Dr Tim Sonnex
(Doctor) and David Butler (Physiotherapist).

1990 -1997

Yeovil Town 1995-96

The Yeovil Years 1990 -1997

As the 1990-1991 season kicked off, the Daily Mail's confidence in the magazine allowed us to publish monthly and we were pleased with the reception the publication had received from the football world. The Non League Football Yearbook with Vauxhall sponsorship had also featured encouragingly in the WH Smiths' book ratings and we knew the game outside the Football League had an enthusiastic following.

John's football continued developing fast and he was selected for Torbay, Devon and South West trials with reasonable success and before the end of the season was invited to train at Torquay United. During the hectic 1991-1992 season with Yeovil Town, the magazine Team Talk was establishing itself, the fifteenth edition of the Non-League Club Directory sold well and life seemed to be dominated by football at all levels.

1990-1991 Bryan Moore's Vital Leadership

Since meeting the Yeovil Town club officials when Hungerford Town had played them twice in the FA Cup, I had met Bryan Moore, one of the Somerset club's directors. Their move to Huish Park from their old sloping ground in the town had not been a financial success and apparently the chairman had decided to stand down.

Bryan Moore had taken over and I was flattered when he contacted me early in the new year and asked if I would join the Board. Yeovil Town were one of the most famous Non-League clubs in the country with excellent support and of course a beautiful new ground. I'd been a player, coach, manager, journalist but a director - surely that was very different !

Bryan explained that the club was in severe debt after the move and would be struggling to strengthen its playing squad, but he was determined to build a Yeovil team on and off the field that would at least care for the club, its traditions and of course its future. Each director was expected to chip in the same amount of money, which would be returned at the end of their service with the club. I was thrilled to be part of such a famous sporting institution, especially with a chairman who appeared to be a very genuine man who really loved his Yeovil Town and the game itself.

So I joined the board in mid February, which wasn't really a good time for me, as my hips were giving a lot of pain and I was due to go in for a double operation at the end of the month. After seeing the team draw 1-1 at home to Northwich Victoria I had time for one away game at promotion chasing Barnet, which we lost 2-3 and then I was off to hospital.

Clive Whitehead was manager at the time and senior professionals included Brian McDermott and Steve Rutter, but money was tight and there was definitely a relegation battle ahead. The Chairman asked me to take responsibility for the Directors notes in the programme, which was an enjoyable challenge, but sometimes tough, when results weren't going our way and we were obviously struggling for funds.

1991- 92 Two Great Signings On and Off the Field

The club made two brilliant signings while desperately trying to pull away from the foot of the table. Famous comedian Richard Digance joined the Board and added a breath of fresh air, plenty of smiles and lots of good fund raising schemes, including celebrity dinners and mammoth auctions. On the field the signing of a brilliant young centre half Mark Shail from Worcester City in 1989, proved a perfect partner for Steve Rutter at the centre of the defence.

At the beginning of April, Steve Rutter was asked to take over as Player Manager and Mark Shail was given the captain's arm band. The club finished the season rising from 20th position to the relative mid table security of 14th in the Conference.

I was learning a lot about senior football clubs, their pressures and the wonderful satisfaction and thrills when the team spirit on and off the field brought results. We were safe for the time being, but financially there was still a lot of work to do. Although Yeovil Town had kept their place in the Conference my first full season turned into a real battle on and off the field. The loss made when moving grounds could well have forced the club to close. Steve Rutter had no managerial budget with which to strengthen his squad and the club itself had to raise a massive amount just to pay debts and everyday running costs.

Looking through the 1991-1992 programmes it was obvious that without Richard Digance's incredible fundraising schemes, the non stop work of Chairman Bryan Moore with his dedicated Board of Directors and the full support of the playing staff and the loyal supporters, Yeovil Town certainly wouldn't have been alive to-day. Many clubs have been seen to throw in the towel and just close down, perhaps starting again with a change of name often leaving many a creditor out of pocket.

The players accepted a reduction in bonuses, directors paid for their own food and drink at the club and paid their own expenses when traveling with the team and staying at hotels before away games. Everyone involved in the club submitted all sorts of ideas for fund raising and carried them out throughout the season.

In fact the away games were extremely important as the board and players learned to respect and understand each other and the pressures that they were all facing. Gradually, under Steve Rutter's managerial leadership, the squad forced their way off the bottom of the table. Mark Shail's outstanding season as skipper and centre half alongside his manager, was also an inspiration to the rest of the players. Yeovil Town finished in a superb fifteenth position, which reflected the battling spirit throughout the club.

I had enjoyed my involvement with the programme notes

The Yeovil Years 1991 - 1993

1. Will Yeovil Town survive? (article from Team Talk magazine)

2. Mark Shail and Steve Rutter provided a powerful central defence which inspired the whole squad to to pull together and take the club away from the foot of the table.

3. Richard Digance, a nationally famous comedian, worked incredibly hard with all types of fundraising and was an extremely popular member of the club.

(1991-92) Back row, left to right: Steve Harrower, Peter Conning, Nigel Stevenson, Mark Hervin, Mark Shail, David Fry, Matthew Carr, Nathan Bush, Mark Boulton, Howard Pritchard and Richard Cooper. *Middle Row:* John Flatters (Youth Team Physio), Mickey Spencer, Brian McDermott, Robbie Carroll, Chris Whalley (Community Development Office), Steve Rutter (Team Manager), Paul Wilson (YTS Officer), Paul Batty, Mike McEvoy, Andy Wallace and Tony Farmer (Physiotherapist). *Front Row (all YTS):* Duncan Birrell, Malcolm McPherson, Steve Sivell, Alastair Carruthers, Terry Dades, Paul Dowding and Nick Flory.

The Yeovil Years 1992 -1994

which were not always easy to keep positive and I was proud of my involvement in a massive exercise with Richard Digance, involving as many businesses and individuals as we could attract to the club.

In fact we were eventually successful with these negotiations at minimal cost, but not so successful in ensuring that George Best's promise of opening it, was kept!

1992-1993 Great Cup Run Inspires the Club

From a personal point of view it was fun taking more responsibility at Yeovil, but to keep covering the rest of the country for the publications meant a great deal of travelling. I was helping on the Football Combination Committee as their West Country member and was also watching the Yeovil Reserves and youth team as much as possible as well as the struggling first team home and away. It was a hectic but enjoyable season as Team Talk and the Directory were proving successful and plans were developing for more sporting books. There is no doubt that if I had still been married I couldn't have happily worked so hard.

This season probably created the base from which Yeovil Town's future progress was eventually made. Everyone from President and Chairman to the youngest supporters and the club's youth team, all pulled together and enjoyed the wonderful FA Cup run and the respectable League position. They all knew just how disastrous it could have been without such an emotional dedicated all round effort.

The messages from the Boardroom give an indication as to the feeling within the club. The excitement, pride and enjoyment from the FA Cup run and the improved league position considering the financial pressure suffered for over the last two years, had created a great place in which to enjoy one's football.

This was a special season for Yeovil Town and for me personally, being a member of their Board of Directors at a very difficult time for the club financially. All the hard work of players and staff was rewarded by an inspirational FA Cup run, finishing with a home tie against the famous Arsenal at Huish Park.

To be involved with a Non-League club when they produced away victories at two Football League clubs, and then played hosts to one of the world's most famous clubs, is an experience that remains a thrill for the rest of one's life.

To win 5-2 at Torquay was a dream come true, but then only managing a draw at home to Hereford was a disappointment. However, that was soon forgotten, when a late winner at Edgar Street meant we had qualified for that dream tie in Yeovil. Just imagine the coach trip home - I will never forget it!

In those days the top clubs played their full side in FA Cup ties whoever they were drawn against and all the North London stars were there to be seen on the same pitch as our local heroes.

Yeovil Town's two best players were unavailable. The skipper Mark Shail was suspended and player manager Steve Rutter was injured, so it wasn't surprising that Ian Wright finished with a match winning hat-trick, but Yeovil did score through Paul Batty who had also registered a hat trick at Torquay.

In fact it was the exciting FA Cup exploits that appealed to John Fry, a successful local businessman with absolutely no apparent knowledge or love for the game. After the excitement of winning with a late goal at Hereford United and qualifying for a visit from Arsenal, he made it clear he would like to join this exhilarating atmosphere and successful 'team'. His business experience was obviously welcomed and he let everyone know he was very ambitious!

It was a great season, but there was still a long way to go as far as financial security was concerned. Conference clubs were generally improving on and off the field, could Yeovil Town keep up with them as they worked hard to build financial security?

1993-94 Anti-Climax Leads to Managerial Changes

After the initial burst of enthusiasm from everyone involved with Yeovil Town Football Club, the emotional battle to save the club from a very sad closure, quite naturally lost some of its initial drive. The playing squad hadn't been strengthened with any senior players but a very reasonable start with three wins and three draws was encouraging. However, a very ordinary campaign persuaded player-manager Steve Rutter to concentrate on playing and after Phil Ferns had taken up the reigns for a spell in mid season, the experienced Brian Hall arrived as manager to stop the slide towards relegation.

Without a substantial budget the introduction of some new faces was extremely difficult, but the manager's contacts and experience certainly helped. So, despite some inspirational performances from Steve Rutter and Paul Wilson, the club reached their last five fixtures in 21st place with only the doomed Witton Albion below them.

With the financial situation still severe, a successful Youth Policy could possibly provide local talent and obviously appeal to the local supporters. It might take time but hopefully, the home crowd would understand.

Five wins and a draw in the last seven games provided the safety of nineteenth place, two points ahead of Merthyr Tydfil. It had been a very difficult campaign for everyone concerned on and off the field, but could the club survive another year without increased financial back up. Could we keep up with the ambitious clubs from The Conference ?

The Yeovil Year 1992 -1994

The men who kept Yeovil Town Football Club alive

  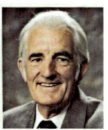   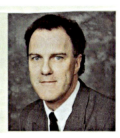

Bryan Moore   Roger Brinsford   Gordon Prosser   Steve Rutter   Alan Skirton   Richard Digance

2.
1992-1993
Back row: Neil Coates, Richard Cooper, Paul Nevin, David Coles, Andy Wallace, Phil Ferns, Jeff Sherwood and Mark Shail.

Middle Row: Tommy Taylor, Mike McEvoy, Steve Sivell, Hung Dang, Wayne Dobbins, Paul Batty and Steve Harrower.

Seated: Chris Whalley (Community Development Officer), Paul Wilson (YTS Officer and Player), Steve Rutter (Player Manager), Paul Rodgers (Coach), Tony Farmer (Physio) and John Flatters (Youth Team Assistant).

Front Row (YTS): Paul Dowding, Mark Rolls, Nathan Bush, Matthew Francis and Malcolm McPherson.

3.
1993-1994
Back Row: Paul Sanderson, Andy Wallace, Malcolm McPherson, Richard Cooper, David Coles, Dave Leonard, Nick Flory, Paul Nevin, Andy Bye

Front Row: Steve Sivell, Steve Harrower, Terry Connor, Neil Coates, Tony Farmer (Physio), Steve Rutter (Manager), Paul Rodgers (Coach), Jeff Sherwood, Mickey Spencer, Wayne Dobbins, Andy Gorman.

Insets: Phil Ferns, Nathan Bush, Paul Wilson

The Yeovil Years 1994 -1995

1994-1995 More Changes - then Relegation

The Club's very limited budget underlined the fact that our small hard core of experienced quality players could not be strengthened. This put unfair pressure on our young players who were not ready for Conference Football and some who were just not good enough.

Frustration was spreading, including pockets of disillusioned supporters which made the day to day running of the club at the top of the Non-League pyramid extremely difficult. Bryan Moore worked all hours and the board of directors pooled their ideas regarding fundraising, which obviously wasn't necessarily our natural strengths.

Local business man John Fry, worked hard to increase share sales and helped in the restructured duties of the board. The pressure was showing on manager Brian Hall, and after a disastrous performance at Walton & Hersham in The FA Cup, it was agreed that a managerial change would benefit everyone.

Tiv Lowe and Paul Wilson, backed up by Jeff Sherwood, held the players together while the club advertised for a new manager and the quality of applicants once again underlined what a fine reputation the club had built within Non-League football.

I remember being amazed that John King, who had built a wonderful reputation at Altrincham, came down from Lancashire to talk to Bryan Moore and our committee. It was mutually agreed that he would be too far from home, but it was good to see him and hear what such an experienced football man thought of our club. However, our new manager had an equally impressive record and we all looked forward to Graham Roberts taking up the reigns. It was accepted that with our present squad, even with the inspirational Roberts, we would have difficulty avoiding relegation.

Watching the ex-Tottenham Hotspur captain at work with the players and indeed the supporters and club officials, it was obvious that his reputation plus a positive and friendly attitude, would inspire support throughout the club on and off the field.

Relegation was accepted, but morale was high with a new charismatic manager in charge. Perhaps being a very big, and hopefully successful club, in the traditional Isthmian League, would attract bigger crowds, more success and could finally improve the club's financial situation. Then, perhaps their income could be kept and used to the benefit of the club, rather than being paid back to the bank.

Meanwhile Tony Williams Publications was continuing to develop well in 'the nineties' with terrific support from Non-League enthusiasts James Wright and Steve Whitney plus George Brown and son Michael, before he was snapped up to join the publications department at Coventry City Football Club.

The eighteenth edition of The Non League Directory was once again listed as a best seller by WH Smith and Team Talk monthly magazine, in its third year, was proving very popular throughout Non-League football.

With possibly the country's most enthusiastic Non-League followers working together, it wasn't surprising that new titles kept emerging and to show we weren't too biased some titles even covered senior football!

Just in case I wasn't involved in enough football, I also had great pleasure in coaching a team of youngsters from North Curry, my village just outside Taunton, who had joined the local Sunday league. Mike enjoyed playing in this squad and as the team had started from scratch, every victory or even a draw was celebrated in a very happy village pub!

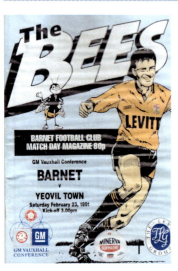

The Yeovil Years 1994 -1995

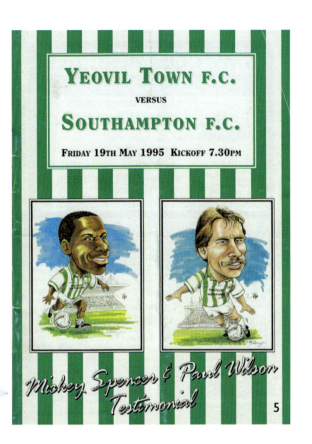

1. 90-91 Prog v Barnet (A)
2. 90-91 Prog v Northwich (H)
3. Prog v Torquay U (a) 92 -93
4. Prog v Crawley T (a) 92 -93
5. YTFC Testimonial 94-95
6. Paul Wilson -1993
7. Yeovil Fans felt like this on more than one occasion in a very happy season
8. Yeovil Town 94 -95
   Back row, left to right: Matthew Leonard, David Morris, David Coles, Peter Mason, Marc Coates and Richard Evans.
   Centre Row: Wayne Dobbins, Matthew Francis, Neil Cordice, Ian Benbow, Nick Flory, Steve Sivel and Mickey Spencer.
   Front Row: Tony Farmer (Physio), Peter Conning, Jeff Sherwood, Brian Hall (Manager), Phil Ferns, Paul Wilson and Anne Read (Physio)

The Yeovil Story 1995 - 96

1995 - 1996 Time to go, as Character of the Club Changes

So John Fry took over as chairman as well as Chief Executive. However, under John's direction, the full board were told less and less of what was going on and soon decisions were made without full consultation. As I was someone with a close working relationship with the Football Association and Non-League football in general, Bryan Moore had realised that I could help the club, but the new chairman made it plain that he didn't agree.

I had obviously made a mistake in rebuking John for his attitude in the Merthyr Tydfil boardroom after we had lost a First Round FA Cup tie. " Our players didn't try, they were a ...... disgrace' he stormed in a packed room.

I explained you didn't rant and rage in your host's boardroom and anyway, if our players didn't care, it was strange that some of them came off the field in tears. In football there are days when you just don't get a result even if you deserve it and we have all got to learn to win graciously and lose with dignity, at least in public.

This went down like a lead balloon and was probably remembered for a long time! So when I suggested I could best serve the new regime with some responsibility on the football side, I was made aware there were no such jobs, and anyway, the Chairman didn't want me on the board as he was going to deal with players, coaching staff, managers, contracts and all footballing matters.

I didn't want to leave Bryan Moore before he had become used to life without the chairmanship, so for two seasons I remained on the board and from reading my programme notes for home matches, I certainly wasn't involved as when I was helping the previous chairman. I left with happy memories of the seasons in which we all shared responsibilities while working hard to keep our wonderful club financially afloat after the move into Huish Park.

The character of the club, originally known to be friendly, sporting and caring for players, management, supporters and board alike, was changing quickly. John seemed to despise football people and football traditions and produced another unfortunate reaction to an FA Trophy defeat in the car park at Kingstonian when a brilliant and unstoppable last minute goal had won the game for the 'K's'.

The disappointment of losing the promotion race to Rushden & Diamonds in 2001 also produced an unfortunate Chairman's outburst at Manager Colin Addison that really did the club's reputation no good whatsoever.

The whole image, inside and from outside the club changed, with the manner of departure that surrounded Graham Roberts, Owen Pickard, Colin Lipiatt, Rob Cousins, Colin Addison, Warren Patmore, Ben Smith and Tony Pennock, confusing for supporters to say the least. All these characters had served the club well and were popular with the regular fans.

These observations were made from my personal experiences during the early years of John Fry's time at the club. I had been as influential as anyone in bringing this apparently successful local businessman to the club and, if Yeovil Town achieved their progress up the divisions through John Fry's business acumen, then he certainly deserves congratulations from all Yeovil Town supporters.

To have competed in The Football League Division One in season 2013-2014 was a superb achievement and obviously the club's historic rise reflects well on the chairman. I sincerely hope that Yeovil Town will be happy and successful in the future, as I enjoyed some exciting seasons with the club, made some great friends and have wonderful memories.

Yeovil Town 1995-96

Back row, left to right: Les Hornby, Chris White, Martin St Hilaire Tony Pennock, Warren Patmore, Lee Francis and Chris Seymour.
Centre Row: Tony Farmer (Physio), Wayne Farnell-Jack, Andy Flory Danny Burwood, Nick Williams, Lee Groves, Rhys Hamer and Anne Read (Assistant Physio).
Front Row: Paul Wilson, Kevin Dillon, Mickey Engwell, Graham Roberts(Player-Manager) Nick Burton and Graham Kemp.

The Yeovil Years 1995 - 96

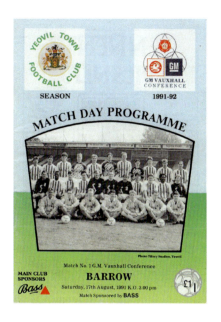
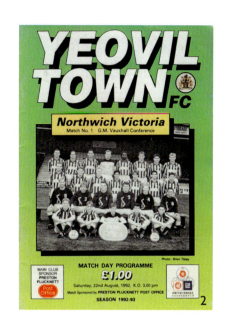
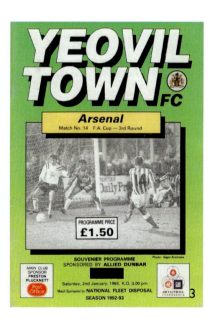
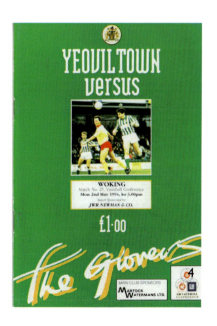
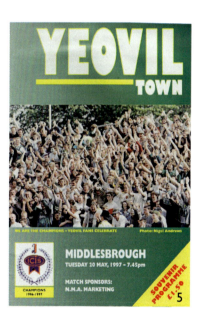

1. 91-92 v Barrow

2. Northwich Victoria 92 -93

5. 96-97 v Middlesborough

3. 92-93 v Arsenal

4. 93-94 Prog v Woking

The Yeovil Years 1996 - 97

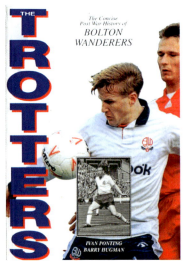

With Yeovil Town drawn away in the FA Cup 2001 I had the pleasure of a week end in Lancashire, a dinner out with Yeovil supporters and Roger Hunt and, of course, meeting my lifetime hero Nat Lofthouse at the match on Saturday.

The Bolton Wanderers book, being the only one I ever compiled for the Football League, was assisted by Nat Lofthouse and, so I'm told, was appreciated by the club.

1.
Yeovil at Bolton 2001
Left to right:
Non-League Media Chief Executive Steve Ireland, Paddy Mullen Yeovil Town scout, Steve Thompson (Yeovil Coach), Bolton Wanderers Chief Executive, Roger Hunt, T.W., Colin Addison and Brian King Non-League Paper Distribution Manager.

2.
Yeovil 1996-19 97
Back row: (left to right) Rob Cousins, Kevin Braybrook, Tony Pennock, James Smith, Dean Birkby, Chris White
Middle row: Terry Cotton (Assistant Manager), Lee Groves, Jamie Laidlaw, Chris Seymour, Jerry Gill, Tony Pounder, Leroy Whale,
Terry Hardwell (Physio)
Front Row: Warren Patmore, Graham Kemp, Graham Roberts (Player Manager), Mickey Englwell, Lee Harvey

Those were the days

This week's best-sellers — OBSERVER 22/

Books
1. The Official FA non league club directory 1998, Tony Williams ed (Tony Williams Publications, pb, £16.95)
2. European football — A fan's handbook — The rough guide, Peterjon Cresswell and Simon Evans (Rough Guides, pb, £14.99)
3. Ashes Summer, Nasser Hussain & Steve Waugh (Collins Willow, hb, £14.99)
4. Complete handbook of pro basketball 1998, Zander Hollander ed (Signet (US), pb, £6.95)
5. The greatest footballer you never saw — The Robin Friday Story, Paul McGuigan and Paolo Hewitt (Mainstream, pb, £9.99)
6. Benson & Hedges Cricket Year (1996/97), David Lemmon ed (Bloomsbury, hb, £20.00)
7. The Football Business, David Conn (Mainstream, hb, £14.99)
8. Build a bonfire — How football fans united to save Brighton and Hove Albion, Stephen North and Paul Hodson (Mainstream, hb, £14.99)
9. Official Rugby union club directory 1997-98, Stephen McCormack ed (Tony Williams Publications, pb, £14.99)
10. Danny Blanchflower — Biography of a visionary, Dave Bowler (Gollancz, hb, £16.99)

Videos
1. When we were kings (Poly... £14.99)
2. Living with Lions (PNE Video, £14.99)
3. Forever Blue — Official History of Chelsea FC (BMG Video, £12.99)
4. Classic Celtic (PNE Video, £12.99)
5. The roar of the Lions (Sky Sports/Fox, £12.99)
6. 1997 Giro D'Italia — Gotti il Incredibile! (2 video set) (World Cycling Productions, £21.99)
7. Highlights of the 1997 Tri Nations Series (Festival Video, £22.99)
8. ReWrighting the Record — Ian Wright (Arsenal FC/PNE, £12.99)
9. Chicago Bulls 1996-97 NBA championship season (NBA Video, £10.99)
10. Australia vs West Indies 1996/97 (ACB Video, £26.99)

Lists compiled by Sportspages: 94-96 Charing Cross Road, London, 0171 240 9604 & St Ann's Square, Manchester, 0161 832 8530

Trivia Teaser: 1967 — QPR 3 West Brom 2.

THIS WEEK'S TOP 10 SPORTS BOOKS
— Greg Wood

1. **The Official FA Non-League Club Directory 1998**, edited by Tony Williams (Tony Williams Publications, paperback, £16.95)
2. **European Football – A Fan's Handbook – The Rough Guide**, Peterjon Cresswell and Simon Evans (Rough Guides, paperback, £14.99)
3. **Ashes Summer**, Nasser Hussain and Steve Waugh (Collins Willow, hardback, £14.99)
4. **Complete Handbook of Pro Basketball 1998**, edited by Zander Hollander (Signet US, paperback, £6.95)
5. **The Greatest Footballer You Never Saw – The Robin Friday Story**, Paul McGuigan and Paolo Hewitt (Mainstream, paperback, £9.99)
6. **Benson & Hedges Cricket Year (1996/97)**, edited by David Lemmon (Bloomsbury, hardback, £20.00)
7. **The Football Business**, David Conn (Mainstream, hardback, £14.99)
8. **Build a Bonfire – How Football Fans United To Save Brighton And Hove Albion**, Stephen North and Paul Hodson (Mainstream, hardback, £14.99)
9. **Official Rugby Union Club Directory 1997-98**, edited by Stephen McCormack (Tony Williams Publications, paperback, £14.99)
10. **Danny Blanchflower – Biography Of A Visionary**, Dave Bowler (Gollancz, hardback, £16.99)

Chart compiled by Sportspages, 94-96 Charing Cross Road, London (0171 240 9604) and St Ann's Square, Manchester (0161 832 8530).

North Curry, Taunton, Somerset TA3 6LE
Fax: 0823 490281   Tel: 0823 490080

TOP TEN DECEMBER BESTSELLERS
1. Non-League Club Directory 1997 edited by Tony Williams (TW Publications, paperback, £16.95).
2. A Year in the Life of Frankie Dettori by Frankie Dettori (Heinemann, hardback, £15.99).
3. Dark Trade — Lost in Boxing by Donald McRae (Mainstream, hardback, £14.99).
4. The European Football Yearbook 1996/97 edited by Mike Hammond (Sports Projects, paperback, £22.95).
5. Dream On — A Year in the Life of a Premier League Club by Alex Fynn and H Davidson (Simon & Schuster, hardback, £14.99).
6. The Complete Handbook of Pro Basketball 1996 edited by Zander Hollander (Signet USA, paperback, £5.95).
7. The NHL Official Guide and Record Book 1996/97 (National Hockey League, paperback, £15.95).
8. The Non-League Football Year Book 1996/97 edited by Kerry Miller and James Wright (Paper Plane, paperback, £15.99).
9. McIlvanney on Boxing by Hugh McIlvanney (Mainstream, hardback, £15.99).
10. Tennent's Lager Scottish Football League Review 1996/97 (Scottish Football League, paperback, £5.95).

List compiled by SPORTSPAGES BOOKSHOPS 94-96 Charing Cross Road, London, 0171-240-9604 & St Ann's Square, Manchester, 0161-832-8530.

North Curry 1996 - 97

Tragedy made me realise how special people are

At a time when it is popular for the English to run themselves down and be self-critical at every opportunity thanks to a media that highlights every sordid, brutal or plainly despicable occurrence, we probably fail to accept that the vast majority of our friends and neighbours are very normal and often very special human beings.

Last week in Taunton, just before being admitted to Musgrove for a second replacement hip operation, I heard about the death of young footballer, Daniel Boddy, whom I helped coach at North Curry Football Club. A very grim few days were in prospect, but I have had one of the most positive weeks of my life. It underlined the depth of really good people who are all around us every day of our lives and usually not in the headlines.

I have just experienced an amazing week in the Taunton area. My faith in human nature, its sense of humour, dedication to duty and all-round team spirit was highlighted in Musgrove's Gould Ward, and the outstanding quality of character shown by the youngsters of North Curry at Daniel Boddy's funeral was of the highest possible standard.

The cheerful politeness and kind professionalism of hospital staff, who often have to cope with awkward situations when dealing with the sick and infirm, was an inspiration to us all and it certainly helped us make light of our minor aches and pains.

Perhaps this particular ward was well led but you could sense the team spirit through the senior staff, junior nurses, catering and cleaners, the surgeons and senior doctors themselves.

Possibly, thanks to their example, the dozen or so fellow patients who passed through the ward during my week, were also wonderful, cheerful and positive company. There's nothing much wrong with the NHS here and I appreciated the efforts made so I could be discharged in time to attend the funeral in North Curry.

As chairman/coach to the football side I had also seen Dan grow up and develop into a really popular and lovely lad who was literally everyone's friend. I had missed the harrowing week in North Curry leading up to the funeral. Richard Perry, who virtually runs the playing side of the club, although terribly distressed himself, had held the club together and helped everyone bond magnificently to face the day with a positive and quite outstanding display of inner strength.

The funeral was attended by more than 600 people and was extremely well-conducted, but the highlight was provided by the four young friends of Dan who came forward to speak about him with genuine loving care and affection laced with the humour, which had always been present in their relationships.

The courage and character shown by Shawn Sutton, Ali Brown, Mel Quinn and club skipper Karl Deans, when they stood in front of a large emotional congregation and gave their clear, strong and very moving stories of Dan, is surely an indication there is a huge untapped source of real English character throughout the country which is lying dormant, just ready to rise to the right occasion or take any initiative available to them.

If I just believed the media, I would never know about the characters within Gould Ward or the incredible potential of the youngsters who rose to the occasion in a very ordinary village, but I know I am very proud to be a small part of these lads' football club and I know the village of North Curry was uplifted by a very special funeral.

In 1966 when England won the World Cup, the feel-good factor throughout the country created a spirit in which the country's productivity broke all records.

We were proud of ourselves and we made the most of the pride we all shared.

Well, this week despite a new hip I feel terrific and although this won't help the country much, I dare say publicity for the thousands of ordinary people like the Gould Ward team and the village youngsters could just make a difference, so let's all be positive.

TONY WILLIAMS
North Curry

from the Taunton Times

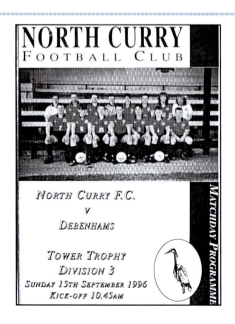

NORTH CURRY FOOTBALL CLUB

10th Year Celebration

Sunday 26th June 6.00pm-10.30pm

at

The Village Hall

With Guest Stars

'Chas 'n' Dave'

and

Roger Hunt (England World Cup Winner, Liverpool)
Neil Webb (Nottm Forest, Manchester United, England) & Colin Addison (Famous Manager)

Pig Roast • Full Bar • Special Raffle • Disco

Tickets only £10.00

2000 - 2017

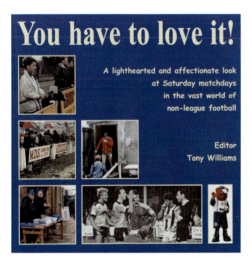

111

2000 Onwards

The new century brought some exciting plans for the promotion of Non-League football. Our editorial team had worked hard to produce over 100 Team Talk magazines and the interest shown by the experienced London journalist David Emery was encouraging and we could see the chance of introducing new Non-League publications together.

David had worked with 'Sport First', an all sport Sunday newspaper which had given good coverage to Non-League football. Having seen the success of Team Talk and the popularity of the Non-League game, he suggested they should publish a purely Non-League paper, but his idea was turned down and David stepped away from his editorial position.

We had enjoyed a spectacular 21st edition of the FA Non-League Club Directory and the annual in 2000-2001 contained a massive 1,056 pages and was once again a best seller. The editorial contributors really enjoyed their work and a superb group of photographers had formed themselves into a happy 'team'. They enjoyed touring the Non-League clubs, although knowing there was little chance of payment, but every chance of a warm welcome wherever they went. They all really seemed to enjoy a super team spirit amongst their mates and loved their annual get togethers at Wembley plus the occasional Team Talk and Non-League Directory parties!

David Emery had realised the size of the Non-League football world in the country and we could all see how the top of our pyramid was strengthening. Two clubs could soon be promoted into The Football League and half the Conference clubs were now playing with full time professionals.

After battling to promote Non-League football with our annual Directory and monthly magazine, here was a chance to be part of a 'Non-League Media' a company floated on the AIM market in Fleet Street. The Non-League Paper on Sundays would back up the monthly 'Team Talk' which had recently celebrated its 100th edition and The Non-League Club Directory which was in its 23rd year.

Ted Croker, the Football Association Chief Executive had originally encouraged us to produce a Non-League annual and promised FA support and encouragement. He would surely have been pleased with the possibilities of these Non-League publications that could really promote their special levels of the national game.

Another much appreciated supporter at this time was Minister of Sport Kate Hoey who encouraged the wealthy television companies to help grass routes football and indeed supported us with personal appearances at our celebrations.

To celebrate the 100th edition of Team Talk we invited friends of the company to join us on the Thames for an afternoon riverboat trip down the Thames with accompanying Jazz Band. Unfortunately I was struck down in hospital with a freak nose bleed which lasted two weeks, so Michael stepped in to host a very successful and enjoyable celebration for many much appreciated friends who had given us great support.

As the 1999-2000 season kicked off we were pleased to welcome a young Non-League footballer who was playing at centre half for Sutton United. Stuart Hammonds joined to work as Assistant Editor to Steve Whitney on Team Talk magazine. Michael also returned having enjoyed a spell as Publications and Programme Editor at Coventry City and had also worked with Ecom Sport, so was looking after the web site.

Our awards lunch in 2000 was attended by Kenny Dalglish and The Ministry of Sport's representative Philip Chamberlain. While sales of the Directory at Sports Pages, the famous London Sports Book shop, once again proved impressive and very exciting.

The FA Non-League Club Directory was officially the No1 in the top sports book bestsellers in the first five weeks after publishing. It beat Steve Redgrave's book in the first week and in the second it actually sold more than David Beckham's autobiography!!

Those were the days!

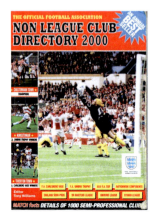 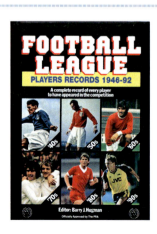 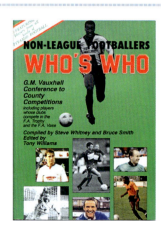

2000 Onwards

100th Team Talk cover

Kate Hoey with award winning manager Martyn Roger

TW Publications in the heart of North Curry

2001 - 2002

Non-League Media plc was developing happily, while promoting the massive world of football below the Football League. Some pressure was obviously taken off our team working in Somerset and 'The Non-League Magazine' a new larger monthly production, with 84 pages and at £2.95p just 45p more expensive, was welcomed as an attractive and very professional publication at the start of the 2001-2002 season

With Stuart Hammond a true Non-League football man at the helm, the magazine was in good hands with the experienced journalistic knowledge of David Emery and my Non-League pedigree available if needed.

I found it a great relief being able to concentrate on traveling up and down the country with time to watch more football than ever before. Tiverton Town and Yeovil Town were still favourites but Porthleven's FA Vase run was exciting and a return to Guernsey for a celebration week-end with 'Happy Histon', who had won our Fair Play award, was enjoyed by everyone involved. Histon qualified as winners as the FA Trophy level club who had received least yellow and red cards in their league programme during the season.

Interesting to note how some club fortunes have changed since the beginning of the century. Crawley Town and Hereford United played Tiverton Town and have since left the Non-League scene in different directions, while Rushden & Diamonds' wonderful years at the top sadly didn't last and Aldershot Town are still working their way back up the pyramid.

The first year working with Non-League Media Plc was enjoyable and The Non-League Paper proved to be a great success. The up market 'Team Talk' boosted the image of Non-League football and as Sky Television was becoming more and more influential, perhaps they would also promote the pleasure available in football played at Non-League levels.

Our 'sister' magazine 'She Kicks' was also welcomed by the ever increasing number of enthusiasts involved with woman's football and James Wright produced a popular weekly Newsdesk and an Annual.

Our Non-League Club Directory increased in pages to 1088, with two of the most knowledgable and enthusiastic Non-League journalists, Steve Whitney and James Wright, backed by House Editor George Brown. They were all still as keen as ever and the 24th edition of the Non-League Club Directory once again proved popular.

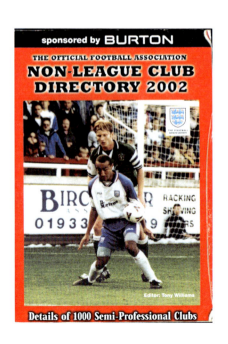

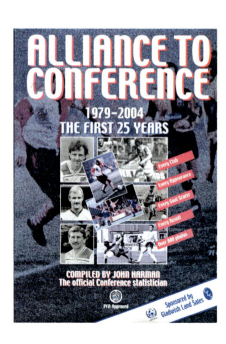

2001 - 2002

The continual development of the Football Conference saw more of their members become full time and the Football League were under constant pressure to introduce 'two up and two down' between the Conference and Division Two.

The Football League clubs voted on the idea which was turned down by 71-1 (thank you for your vote Wycombe Wanderers)! Ongoing discussions over regional feeders for The Conference appeared to suggest a deal with the Southern and Northern Premier leagues, much to the anger of the Isthmians who understandably felt they should also be feeding Non-League football's top competition.

With Wembley Stadium being rebuilt, the FA Trophy and FA Vase Finals were played at Villa Park. The thrill of a Final and the fact that Yeovil Town under the guidance of Gary Johnson beat Stevenage Borough, gave the Yeovil fans a memorable day in Birmingham.

I was still enjoying my involvement with The North Curry village team on Sundays and as a pre season warm up, we enjoyed a week-end in Cornwall playing the friendly, and after their FA Vase heroics, quite famous, Porthleven club!

Before the 2003 edition of the Non-League Club Directory was published, the sad news had filtered down to us here in Somerset that 'Non-League Media plc' had suffered internal company problems, nothing to do with football, which had forced the company into administration.

This was extremely worrying to our West Country editorial team, who had accepted the introduction of a bigger and more professional magazine taking over from Team Talk, but now feared for the future of the 25th edition of The Directory.

Happily, David Emery was able to place the successful Non-League paper in the hands of Greenway Media, a sister company run with Chris Ingram, Chairman of Woking FC. While responsibilities for The Directory reverted to Tony Williams Publications, but there was no new magazine.

The 'Team Talk' Team

Tony Williams   Michael Williams

James Wright   Mike Fairbairn

Adrian Barber   Ken Bithell

2002 - 2003

A memorable season for senior Non-League football welcomed the opportunity for two clubs to qualify for Football League membership instead of just the champions. A Play-Off system was introduced and featured Morecambe, Doncaster Rovers, Chester City and Dagenham & Redbridge at the end of the season

However, the Conference season was dominated by a superb Yeovil Town squad which had been put together by David Webb, developed by Colin Addison and lovingly nurtured by a dedicated and understanding Manager Gary Johnson. If these three managers had all added their vital characteristics to the squad, one vital influence who remained all through was Steve Thompson, the permanent right hand man who proved to be the Non-League game's most successful coach.

The Yeovil squad was one of the best ever built at the top of the Non-League world, coach Thompson had kept the spirit intact as two managers failed to provide what the chairman demanded. However, the club's owner Jon Goddard-Watts, of Screwfix fame, ensured the financial backing was available to cover the club's working losses, allowing Yeovil Town to build a wonderful squad that eventually took 'The Glovers' into the Football League.

Nine Yeovil Town players won international caps, with two Welshmen missing selection through injury and Scotsman Michael McIndoe (The Conference Player of the Year), not selected for Scotland as he wasn't playing for a Scottish club. Congratulations to all involved for an historic season.

After such an unfortunate collapse of our exciting ideas for developing the promotion of Non-League football publications, we settled down to ensuring the Directory continued and sales were consistent. We also added a Non-League diary and a Non-League poster highlighting the re-structured national pyramid of leagues. Since the annual publication was launched in 1978, we had appreciated the sponsorship support and encouragement from Rothmans, Duripanel, Safestand, Compact Grandstands, Vauxhall Motors, Lucozade Sport, Sports Marketing Systems and Burtons the Tailors.

Before TW Publishing took over in 1986, professional support was also enjoyed from original publishers Queen Anne Press, Playfair Publishing, Rothmans Publishing and Newnes Books. So the involvement of Ladbrokes as new sponsors in 2002 was welcomed and the company's outstanding interest in Non-League football impressed everyone involved. The company associated itself with The Ladbrokes Fair Play Non-League Club which they enthusiastically helped to promote through the Ladbrokes FairPlay Magazine.

Another special addition to our publications was the introduction of 'You Have to Love It' This was a collection of photographs from our loyal team of photographers, illustrating many aspects of Non-League football, including the humour and spirit we all enjoy so much.

So despite the frightening collapse of the new company, it appeared that the spirit of Non-League football was still very much alive and kicking athletically! We had one more new idea in which the clubs could show their own Non-League knowledge, so clubs were sent a poster on which they could answer some Non-League questions. The best eight entries received were then invited to a Midland hotel for a Friday evening quiz before the Villa Park Trophy Final on the Saturday. The final evening saw Altrincham, Barnet, Forest Green Rovers, Guiseley, Hertford Town, Ilfracombe Town, Rugby United and Winchester City qualify for The Final, which was won eventually by Forest Green Rovers who beat Altrincham by just one point.

The FA Trophy and FA Vase Finals were still being played away from Wembley and the senior knock-out competition proved to be a bit different, as no Conference club reached the Semi-Finals. Burscough (NPL) beat Aylesbury United (Isthmian League) 1-1 and 1-0 and Tamworth (Southern League) beat Havant & Waterlooville (Southern Lg) 1-1 and 1-0. Then in front of 14,265 at Villa Park, Burscough won the Final 2-1.

Thank You Ladbrokes

Our promotion of Non-League football, publicity appeared to have taken a knock with its monthly magazine disbanded. So it was encouraging for all of us to see the welcome and support that our new publications received from the football public. Despite the disappointment of The Non-League Media plc collapse Ladbrokes' support had given us the confidence to continue with The Directory, The Fair Play Club, The Diary, The Pyramid Poster a National Non-League Club Quiz and the new **'Ladbrokes FairPlay Magazine.'**

'Fairplay' was published in 2004 and, as its name suggests, we were attempting to show our national game wasn't losing its principles and standards.

We were very lucky that Ladbrokes, the famous 'bookies' were extremely keen to be linked with Fair Play in football and they considered the magazine an ideal way in which to promote the good aspects of our national game and to be seen to care.

2002 - 2003

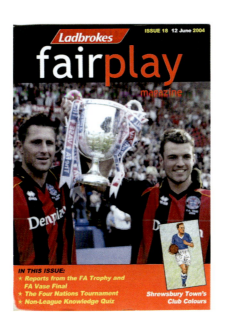
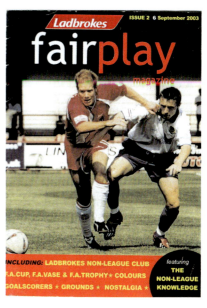
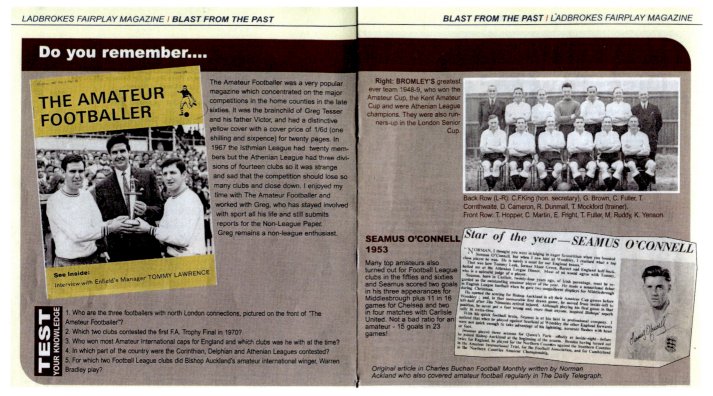

Ladbrokes's 'Fair Play' magazine was one of the most enjoyable to compile. Mike and I were joined by George Brown, Tim Hales' wife Robbie for admin and old friend Forbes Chapman on advertising

2003 - 2004

From a domestic point of view, I was enjoying my football as much as ever and it was good to see The North Curry village club developing well, with the newly opened village Coffee Shop also providing the opportunity to help another excellent addition to village life.

Grandson Sam, Katy's son, was showing a love of the game and was playing his football in the Exeter Sunday Youth League. As he was the only boy amongst six grandchildren his enjoyment of the great game was particularly encouraging!

Michael, was also enjoying a full and varied life within football at all levels, was Loddiswell's General Manager and enjoyed being involved with the squad that won a divisional final of the South Devon Football League. I was busy with my coaching with North Curry on Sundays, which completed a very full weekly football programme.

Another busy season was usually based in the West Country but FA Cup, FA Trophy and The FA Vase ties brought rare, but enjoyable visits to Ledbury Town, Hamworthy United, Exmouth Town, Chippenham Town, Chipping Norton Town, Paulton Rovers, Mangotsfield Town, Swindon Supermarine, Leamington, Mossley, Redditch United, Stafford Rangers, Bideford, Winchester City and Canvey Island.

With the redeveloping work still unfinished at Wembley Stadium, the Trophy and Vase Finals were both played in the West Midlands and provided historic victories for Hednesford Town and Winchester City.

The first ever National League Systems Cup gave 22 of the 24 Level Four clubs an exciting knock out competition with the thrilling reward for the eventual winners, who would be nominated as England's representative in the 2004-2005 UEFA competition. This provided a new challenge for players at Level Four but the players had to be between 19-33 years old and never having signed a professional playing contract.

After five successful seasons in charge of the England Semi-Professional squad, John Owens had stood down and the ex-Stevenage Borough manager Paul Fairclough took over and found availability of Conference players not always easy to achieve. But this was the beginning of a long and successful career looking after the young English talent passing through the Non-League world.

Conference clubs had given John Owens a hard time and the new manager found their attitude no better. Team selection was difficult for the newly named 'National Game XI.

His first two internationals were against full time Under 23 professionals from Belgium and Italy and it wasn't until the third game, against Scotland, that the patched up squad recorded a 3-1 victory - a fine reward for the new manager's hard work.

Spreading the three fixtures throughout the season had upset the club managers who didn't want to lose their players in mid season, so an end of season tournament would surely have been more popular with everyone. At T.W.Publications we had concentrated on The FairPlay magazine, sponsored by Ladbrokes and it developed into a very enjoyable and popular publication containing some original features.

A wonderful party for Sam and some of my special football friends. Douggie Webb (centre) with son Neil and Roger Hunt, all with partners. Having played with Roger in an FA XI during my RAF days and Douggie in Reading Reserves, we had all kept in touch for many years and seeing Neil's wonderful career develop was an extra bonus.

I had been left well behind and was very proud of these friends, as Roger of course was a World Cup winner with England in 1966, Douggie scored 100 goals for Reading and Neil became a full England International and also scored a vital goal in an FA Cup Final. Thanks for coming lads!

2003 - 2004

LADBROKES FAIRPLAY MAGAZINE / COACHING

GOALKEEPING
CATCHING THE HIGH CROSS

In each issue we are including coaching features illustrated by photos taken by our team of photographers for our old magazine Team Talk and the Non-League Directory over the last fifteen seasons. We hope that many players in these photos will jog your memories as well as illustrating interesting coaching points.

Confident Goalkeeping inspires defences "lifts the morale of the whole team" depresses the opposition.

So a goalkeeper with a 'clean pair of hands' or in other words, a keeper who doesn't fumble the centres, is confidant enough to call loudly to claim the cross and doesn't flap at the high balls, is often worth a goal start to your team.

This week's coaching tips show goalkeepers confidently taking responsibility for the high corners, free kicks, shots or lobs into the box.

1. Above - With eyes firmly on the ball and hands safely plucking this lob out of the air, Tilbury's James Nicholls ends an attack in an F.A.Cup tie at Great Yarmouth in perfect style.
Photo: Neil Thaler 1999

Nos 2, 3 & 4 are wonderful examples of keepers taking the high cross at full stretch which gives the opposition absolutely no chance at all and boosts the confidence of his fellow defenders.

In No 2 Colwyn Bay keeper Roberts foils the Blyth attack at Croft Park.
Photo: Graham Brown

No.3 (left) shows Lee Martin of Macclesfield Town gathering safely against Altrincham.
Photo: Keith Clayton

And No 4 is a photo taken at Stamford where Chelmsford City goalkeeper Paul Catley is in complete command. Photo: Gavin Tutcher

No 4
of an illustrated coaching series from
adidas

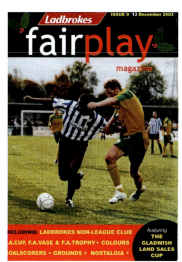

OUR THANKS TO LADBROKES

This, the eighteenth edition of the Fair Play magazine signals the end of the first season for Ladbroke's Fair Play club members who have had the opportunity to watch the England team at Darlington, Shrewsbury and in the Highlands of Scotland, join the dinner parties before attending the F.A.Vase and F.A.Trophy Finals and take part in,or watch, the non-league knowledge inter club quiz finals.

Ladbrokes have enabled a lot of real football fans to make the most of their season and the company has also promoted Fair Play once again by rewarding the clubs throughout the country who have proved to be the most sporting in their respective leagues.There will be some very smart clubs proudly wearing the new strips supplied by Ladbrokes to all regional winners.

We have been thrilled with the way the famous bookmakers have helped the level of the game we care about so much, and hopefully any of you who enjoy the occasional bet will have chosen Ladbrokes to have given you a chance of a little bonus.

From a football point of view, our season has been dominated by the restructuring of the non-league pyramid and most clubs are looking forward to an exciting season after a little bit of rest in the summer.

We will be writing to all the Ladbrokes Fair Play club members about our plans for next season but as you will see elsewhere in this magazine, new membership costs thirty pounds and for those renewing for another year the fee is reduced to twenty pounds.

At a time when the excellent Non-League Paper gives our level of the game such good publicity we are particularly thrilled that Ladbrokes have given us the confidence, through their support, to develop our ideas and for the next three hectic months we will once again be working on The Non-League Club Directory, Non-League Diary and our new Pyramid Poster which all have to be ready early in the coming season.

Finally, we hope you have enjoyed the season and will be able to re-charge the batteries in the summer. Let's hope the European Championships prove successful, entertaining, sporting and an inspiration to all the rest of the country's football people.

TW.

2004 - 2005

The introduction Of Conference North and Conference South saw The Northern Premier, Isthmian and Southern League reduced in quality. But with two clubs joining the Football League from The Conference every year, the incentive for progress really put the pressure on Club Chairmen and their 'money men' throughout the Non-League pyramid.

Our Non-League Diary proved popular and got another very hectic season off to a good start. We also published a special book to celebrate The Alliance/Conference first 25 years and our 27th edition of the Non-League Club Directory.

The first F.I.F.A. International Under 21 tournament in Guernsey gave me a chance to meet some old friends and also see how the Island's involvement in senior football was continuing to develop successfully. This was the first professional tournament held on the Island and was contested by Boca Juniors (Argentina), Paris Saint Germain, Glasgow Rangers and Japan, the World Under 21 champions!

I thoroughly enjoyed another season dominated mostly by visits to South Western clubs and apart from regulars such as Tiverton Town, Bridgwater Town, Taunton Town and the progressive Forest Green Rovers, there were more visits to Downton, Tavistock Town, Frome Town, Chard Town, Mangotsfield United and Bodmin Town who all proved that Association Football was still just as popular as the traditional West Country Rugby.

Tiverton Town enjoyed their FA Cup campaign with a 4-1 victory over Newport County and a visit from Doncaster Rovers and I enjoyed visits to Canvey Island, Didcot Town, Histon, Hednesford Town, Hucknall Town, Northwich Victoria and Redditch United.

Yeovil Town were of course beginning to enjoy life as a Football League club, so their traditional, much feared giant killing reputation in the FA Cup, wasn't seen in quite the same light. However, it was still good to see 'The Glovers' entertain Bolton Wanderers in The Football League Cup and it brought back memories of Wanderers last minute cup victory at Burnden Park in 2001.

The FA Trophy and FA Vase were still without their end of season climax at Wembley, and sadly, the Conference clubs appeared to be re-acting to the loss of a possible glamorous end of season at the famous stadium. No Conference club qualified for The FA Trophy Final for three years!

The importance of challenging for a place at the top of the Non-League pyramid, and then the prospect of challenging for a Football League place appeared to be putting a frightening strain on some clubs finances. A number of clubs appeared to be spending more than they could afford and the reliance on local talent no longer appeared to be adequate to keep up with the high flyers.

Barnet had won The Conference Championship by a massive twelve points under the superb leadership of Paul Fairclough, but the names in the top seven in the final Conference table just showed how the membership of the top competition outside the Football league had changed since the early Alliance days.

Only Stevenage Borough and Morecambe hadn't already played in The Football League and of course they didn't have long to wait! Exeter City in their short spell as a Non-League FA Cup challenger, actually brought great publicity to the Conference when they drew their Third Round FA Cup tie 0-0 against Manchester United at Old Trafford.

The first FA National League Systems Cup, which had been played over two seasons. came to a climax at The Abbey Stadium Cambridge, where The Mid Cheshire League became the first winners by beating The Cambridge County League 2-0.

Interesting to note that in the 2006 Non-League Club Directory we expressed a hope that The Football Association would recognize standards of sportsmanship were decreasing. A national survey had listed the three attributes most treasured by the British public:-

> Firstly: Freedom of Speech
>
> Second: The defence of our country in 1940
>
> Third : A sense of Fairness and Fair Play

Perhaps the Football Association and the Press would realise we don't want to see cheats prosper or glorified, especially on our sports fields.

Were we to expect improvement in the next ten years? Or would the possibility of financial rewards prove more attractive than fair play?

FA Trophy Finals 2001-2006

Season	Ground	Finalists		Finalists		Att	Result
2001	Villa Park	Canvey Island	(Isthmian)	Forest Green R	(Conference)	10,007	1-0
2002	Villa Park	Yeovil Town	(Conference)	Stevenage B	(Conference)	18,809	2-0
2003	Villa Park	Burscough	(N.P.L.)	Tamworth	(Southern)	14,265	2 1
2004	Villa Park	Hednesford T	(Southern)	Canvey Island	(Isthmian)	6,635	3 2
2005	Villa Park	Grays Athletic	(Conf South)	Hucknall T	(Conf North)	8,116	1-1, 6-5 ps
2006	Upton Park	Grays Athletic	(Conference)	Woking	(Conference)	13,997	2-0

Conference Final Top Eight in 2004-2005

	P	W	D	L	Goals	Pts
Barnet	42	26	8	8	90-44	86
Hereford United	42	21	11	10	68-41	74
Carlisle United	42	20	10	9	74-37	73
Aldershot Town	42	21	10	11	68-52	73
Stevenage Borough	42	22	6	14	65-52	72
Exeter City	42	20	11	11	71-50	71
Morecambe	42	19	14	9	69-50	71

2005 - 2006

Another similar season touring the West Country was enjoyable, with visits to Budleigh Salterton, Cirencester Town, Clevedon Town, Dorchester Town, Salisbury City, Street, Wellington and Weston-super Mare, plus more distant clubs such as Birtley Town, Brockenhurst, Evesham United, Merthyr Tydfil and Ossett Town.

Once again the real fun was picking out FA Cup, Trophy or Vase games which brought clubs together from different leagues and backgrounds. Street v Penzance, Merthyr Tydfil v St Blazey, Tiverton Town v Windsor & Eton and Ossett Town v Leamington were all special FA Cup ties for the fans of those clubs and also fascinating for any Non-League enthusiast.

National League Systems Cup

The second bi-annual National League Systems Cup was proving popular and attracted 33 Leagues including representatives from Guernsey, Jersey and The Isle of Man. Having proudly represented The Isle of Man and Guernsey, I found this competition particularly exciting, especially as the winner was to be our representative in a European Tournament.

The new competition gave a genuine lift to the amateur players at Step 7 plus the Islands and I was pleased to attend St Blazey hosting The South Western League's tie against The Jersey Combination, The Guernsey Priaux League who hosted The Reading League at Vale Recreation Football Club and The Dorset Premier League who entertained the Guernsey League.

The Quarter Finals gave me another chance to see the special Guernsey squad and they qualified for a semi-final against The Cambridge League with a 2-0 victory over The South Western League at St Blazey, while The Isle of Man beat The Anglian Combination 3-1 after extra time.

The possibility of an inter Island Final was ruined by The Cambridge League beating Guernsey on penalties after a thrilling 3-3 draw, but The Isle of Man did reach the final with a 2-1 victory over The Kent County League.

The winners of the Final would be asked to represent England in The UEFA Regions Cup and it was The Isle of Man, with a 2-0 victory, who took their place in Group 4, alongside The Czech Republic, Slovakia and the Winners of The Central West Qualifying group.

More memories were resurrected when an invitation was received to attend the Royal Air Forces's Inter Services match against The Army at RAF Uxbridge. Many of my old friends, who I had played with for The Royal Air Force and Icarus, the RAF Officers side, were attending in a wonderful reunion organized by Squadron Leader Peter Cooper, who had done more than anyone else to promote RAF football.

In the 2007 edition of the Non-League Directory it was clear the editorial mood had been severely damaged by the antics we had all watched in the recent World Cup Final, and a few suggestions were made to the games most important characters.

Chairmen:
Instruct your managers to ensure their players don't risk missing important games through stupid, unnecessary bookings and Dismissals.

Managers:
Ensure your teams are respected for their football and tactical skills not their pathetic cheating. Behave with some sort of discipline in the dug out, where supporters (young and old) can hear your language and see your behaviour.

Players:
Make sure you don't give the impression of being the saddest bunch of losers, by screaming at officials, diving whenever touched and losing all respect as you drive supporters away

Youth Coaches:
Make sure the youngsters don't think it clever to copy the cheats.

Referees:
Respond to any clubs attempting to play to the rules in a sporting fashion by ensuring cautions are really deserved, but punish the cheats severely.

The Media:
Praise good sportsmanship and make sure those deliberately fouling or cheating are made to took pathetic for letting their side down and making the game look cheap and unpleasant.

The wonderful family of Non-League Football: can lead the way by making football a happier place for the young referees coming through the system. How about just the captains speaking to The Officials?

2006 - 2007

But the season was kicked off for me by Bishop Auckland's southern tour to play Oxford City and Corinthian-Casuals. The famous North Eastern club had beaten Oxford City 3-0 in the 1906 F.A.Amateur Cup Final and had also beaten Corinthian-Casuals in a Replay at Middlesbrough, after drawing their final at Wembley in front of 80,000 in 1956

The pattern of this football season was much the same. I enjoyed my tour of the West Country with Tiverton Town a mid table club in the Southern Premier Division and Forest Green Rovers establishing themselves as Conference regulars.

It was interesting to attend the launch of E.O.N's four year sponsorship of the FA Cup and my first 'E.O.N. cup tie that season was won 4-0 by Willand Rovers at Chard Town in the Preliminary Round.

It was always good to return to my old club Hungerford Town, and this season they were excited when drawn at home for a Fourth Qualifying Round FA Cup tie against Weymouth.. Hungerford had only reached the First Round Proper once, in 1979, when we had the misfortune to be drawn away to fellow Non-Leaguers and neighbours Slough Town, who burst our bubble with a sound beating.

Record Attendance for FA Vase Final

The FA Vase produced some exciting pairings which I enjoyed in the West Country, before the draw was made on a national basis. Radstock Town took on Bodmin Town, Bideford entertained Corsham Town, Wimborne Town did play Street, another club from the West, in the Fifth Round and a really great Vase tie in Cornwall, saw Truro City beat Newcastle Benfield.

The FA Vase is a very special competition and the four Semi-Finalists this year were AFC Totton (Wessex League) who beat Billingham Synthonia (Northern League) and Truro City (Western League) who beat Curzon Ashton (North West Counties). A very good year for the South West and the entertaining FA Vase Final was the first at The New Wembley.

The Cornish club was on the crest of a wave with good financial backing, manager Dave Leonard had built a squad that was too strong for Division One of The Western League which they had won with 37 victories in 42 games, just one defeat, a goals record of 185-23 and 118 points!

So it wasn't surprising that The FA Vase went to Cornwall, but what was a very welcome surprise was the FA Vase record attendance of 27,754 which beat the previous record of 26,487 in 1989, for the Tamworth v Sudbury Town Final.

Obviously the return to Wembley had given the FA Vase and FA Trophy competitions a much needed boost. Stevenage Borough beat Kidderminster Harriers (both Conference clubs!) 3-1 in the senior knock out competition, also in front of a record Final attendance for The FA Trophy of 53,262. This beat the previous best of 34,842 for the Wycombe Wanderers v Kidderminster Harriers Final in 1993.

I had always taken an interest in The Inter Services competition, ever since I had failed to impress in my game for the Royal Air Force against The Navy, but this season it was interesting to see that the old rivals were meeting each other in The South West Counties Competition along with Cornwall FA and Guernsey FA.

North Curry, the village team I coached on Sundays enjoyed a reasonable season including a couple of interesting fixtures v Rail Madrid and P.Q.R. in the Taunton Sunday League!

The European Challenge Trophy was settling down with England's Under 23s playing against Representative sides from Belgium, Italy and Holland. The competition was played over two seasons and Paul Fairclough's lads had already won 2-0 in Belgium and 3-1 at home to Italy.

This left a third game, at home to Holland at Burton Albion's impressive new Pirelli Stadium in November and after conceding an early goal, an excellent performance gave England the title with a resounding 4-1 victory.

At the end of the season the Four Nations tournament was held in Scotland and the manager's full squad covered themselves in glory, recording three victories without conceding a goal: 5-0 v Eire, 3-0 v Scotland and 3-0 v Wales.

With Wembley Stadium back in business, play-offs now fully accepted, providing a second club promoted to The Football League from the twenty four club Conference, the pressure on managers to gain promotion to the Conference and then to The Football League, had never been greater.

2006 - 2007

As it was the Thirtieth edition of our Non-League Club Directory, we asked some friends who we knew really cared for the Non-League world, to write a few lines for our birthdays !

Dave Bassett:	Ex amateur international and successful Non-League manager.
Barry Bright :	Vice Chairman of the FA and Chairman of The FA Disciplinary Committee
Paul Fairclough:	Successful manager of Stevenage Borough, Barnet and England C
Barry Fry:	A lifetime of experience as a Non-League player, Manager & Director
Roger Hunt:	Non-League with Warrington Town & Devizes Town then a World Cup winner
Dough Insole:	Player with Pegasus & Corinthian-Casuals and Test &Essex cricketer
Tony Jennings:	Hendon, Enfield and England Non-League Captain and Manager
David Miller:	Ex Oxford University Blue and Football correspondent for The Times
Bryan Moore:	Chairman and lifetime supporter of Yeovil Town
Dennis Strudwick:	A Non-League player before Secretary of Southern Lg and Conference
Ron Tarry:	Ex-Player, Coach, Manager, Committee, Chairman and President of Hungerford
Gordon Taylor:	Ex professional player and then Chairman of P.F.A.
Peter Taylor:	Ex Full & Non-League England International and League club manager
Adrian Titcombe:	FA Official and great supporter of Non-League football
Martin Tyler:	Ex Non-League player and top national football commentator
Brian Wakefield:	Ex Great Britain Amateur international goalkeeper

For those real football people to take time to send their special messages, was greatly appreciated by Michael and I. These real Football people have remained true supporters of the game at all levels and we have been honoured to have their support and friendship.

As it was The Directory's thirtieth birthday, I thought it would be a good idea to contact a few of the people I have met through the game who genuinely cared for non-league competitions, and ask them to mention a highlight of their own and also what they hoped for concerning the game at this level in the future.

Mike and I appreciate the time these very busy and respected football people have given on our behalf, and are thrilled that their response is a fine testament to the high regard they have for non-league football.   T.W.

DENNIS STRUDWICK enjoyed a long non-league playing career before becoming Secretary of the Southern League and is now the General Manager of the Football Conference.

I am flattered to have been asked to contribute to the 30th edition of Tony Williams' Non-League Club Directory. Having been able to play the great game for several years (including ten for my home town club, Horsham) and having so far spent 30 years of my working life in football administration, I have been lucky for a long time.

There is no substitute for playing. So to anyone at the crossroads, wondering whether to 'have another season or not', my advice would be, 'play on'. We are all a long time watching.

When the time finally comes to bin the boots, you may want to continue an active role and coach the younger generation(s) of players or, If administration is your forte, and you have innovative ideas, put them to the test with your local club or league. I doubt if many players consider how clean kit, two teams and match officials all arrive at the same time on a given day to play a game on a pitch that has been prepared for their use. And I do not suppose many consider fixture scheduling, unless of course it is to speculate how they could do it better. There is nothing wrong with any of this; why should players give these matters a thought?

But, when playing becomes a thing of the past, it is a good time to put new, young ideas into action. Try it. Invest some time in the game that has given you so much enjoyment. Effect the changes you think are necessary. You will not be sorry, as It has enabled me to prolong the greatest experiences I have gleaned from football such as the friendships and the new ones made along the way.

I would not swap many of the experiences my participation in football has given me, for anything and there is not much I would wish to change. Perhaps, on reflection, there is one thing; I wish The Directory had started 30 years earlier.

Dennis Strudwick

PAUL FAIRCLOUGH a very successful manager with Stevenage Borough, Barnet and England C (England's non-league international squad)

Winning the championship with Barnet was a satisfying moment in my career because of the fact that I had been out of the club scene for a few years and had yet to fulfil my ambition of becoming a football league manager.

Playing Newcastle United in a double header with Stevenage Borough was also thrilling. and each and every time I lead out the England team I am consumed with pride.

Non-League football has grown in strength in many aspects. The quality of performance, stadia and surfaces gets better and better.

My vision would be to see the current Non-League National team (England C) in the Olympic games or Commonwealth games. Obviously there may be a need for a Great Britain team and other nations best non-league players would be part of that team.

Paul Fairclough

PETER TAYLOR is manager of Crystal Palace Football Club who earned Non-League International honours for England having already won four full international caps for his country. He has since become a very successful club and international manager

"Good luck to the Non-League Club Directory in its Thirtieth year. It is still a good read.

I remember my time in non league so well. Great memories, great togetherness with players to players and supporters to players. Everybody felt a part of their club,

The standard is getting better and better and I am sure play-offs and automatic promotion have helped that.

Best wishes to everyone,

Peter Taylor

2006 - 2007

DAVID MILLER played in the Isthmian and Corinthian Leagues and F.A. Amateur Cup competition before becoming one of Britain's most respected national football journalists who received a FIFA Centenary Jules Rimet Award

In the contemporary football world we cannot rely on leadership and integrity from the top. FIFA has been castigated by an American judge for failing to uphold its own slogan of fair play when switching a sponsorship deal to VISA, awarding huge damages in favour of Mastercard. Nor did FIFA see any need for retrospective discipline against Thierry Henry for blatantly cheating in the World Cup against Spain in 2006. For that basic sense of sportsmanship which lies at the heart of the game and is the motivation of the millions who play on anonymous council pitches and parks, we have to rely on human instinct. Fair play is a code that is born in us. Whether it is the three-year-old playing Snap, the eight-year-old playing draughts or the twelve-year-old calling the lines when making the first attempt at tennis, we know what is fair and unfair without being told. It is this sense which during 150 years of organised football has been the bedrock of participation. In this capacity, non-league football is the moral base on which the game survives, never mind how tenuously at times these days in the ambitious pursuit of trophies. Non-League football thrives not on winning trophies, but the simple exhilaration of involvement, on a way of life. While agents, coaches, managers, and some directors at the minority top professional level do so much to damage the beauty of the game, non-league teams are the genuine soul of the sport. May they long survive.

David Miller

DOUG INSOLE was a very good player in senior amateur football and is now an F.A. councillor who was, of course, a Test cricketer and one of the most honoured cricketing administrators in the game.

I played most of my football for Walthamstow Avenue, Cambridge University, Pegasus and Corinthian Casuals in the good (or bad?) old amateur days.

I suppose the highlight of my so-called 'career' was the Casuals/Bishop Auckland Cup Final at Wembley in 1956, but the best match I ever played in was the Varsity match at Tottenham in 1948, which my team Cambridge lost 5-4.

Non-League football these days is very watchable and the overall standard of play is impressive. Tony Williams has supported and promoted the game at this level for yonks and he has made a valuable contribution to what appears to be a very promising future.

Doug Insole

TONY JENNINGS won more modern non-league honours than any other player and also captained and managed the England non-league international squad.

Year 1982 kick-started my departure from playing at semi-pro level. My last season resulted in a second win for Enfield at Wembley, winning the F.A. Trophy, following an earlier success with Hendon in the early seventies, this time for the "F.A. Amateur Cup".

A link with success at club level can be based on good management and team spirit with playing staff being positive. Combine these factors successfully and your side will win more fixtures than they lose, then when drawn in F.A. Cup fixtures your club's belief and confidence will improve more than you would have expected.

But sadly my enjoyment of watching non-league today and the top professionals hasn't increased.

Team managers should take responsibility for their players' attitude towards officials, discourage 'diving' and stress the importance of hard but fair tackling.

This is the least that spectators should expect at any level of the game. Good luck

Tony Jennings

ROGER HUNT scored three goals in England's famous World Cup tournament success in 1966 and will be remembered as one of the eleven heroes in our country's most successful football team of all time.

I am delighted to be asked by Tony Williams to contribute to the 30th Edition of the Non-League Club Directory.

My association with Tony goes back to the late fifties when we were both selected to play for an FA XI against London University.

I am always amazed at the amount of Non-League clubs there are in this country and the number of people who give their support in all kinds of ways.

I have non league football to thank for my chance in the professional game. I was doing National Service in Wiltshire where I played for Devizes Town and also Warrington Town when I was home on leave. From there I signed for Liverpool, which led to a wonderful period of my life in professional football.

I would like to see more players from non league given a chance, instead of the idea that you need to spend millions to be successful.

Best wishes to Tony Williams Publications for their 30th Edition.

Roger Hunt

DAVE BASSETT was skipper of the splendid Wimbledon side that won three consecutive Southern League championships, won silverwear at Wembley and played for England Amateurs before making a name for himself as a top class senior manager and respected media pundit.

We were lucky enough to be at the top of the non-league pyramid at Wimbledon and I will never forget our F.A.Cup ties when we beat First Division Burnley away, and drew with top team Leeds United, also away, before my famous 'own goal' helped them just manage to beat us in the replay. We were proud to be non-league at the time but obviously I have been lucky enough to have served the game at the highest level since then.

I keep an eye on the non-league scene and the standards seem to be improving right the way through the well organised system of leagues. When you think of the number of quality players who have been produced from these competitions it seems wrong that so much money goes out of the country to bring in overseas youngsters who are often no better than our own local talent.

Long may the non-league world flourish and congratulations on your thirtieth edition.

Dave Bassett

ADRIAN TITCOMBE was a leading light in the formation of the F.A.Vase and the negotiations that produced the Alliance and restructuring of senior Non-League football in the seventies. He was also a driving force that gave non-league football an England team to represent them in 1979 and was recognised around the world for leading the teams on to the field at the Wembley Cup Finals.

Having now been associated with The Football Association for over 35 years and for much of that time involved with the game at non-League level, it is no simple matter to identify a single highlight. I suppose the exhilarating performances of the England Semi-Pro team in winning the 1983 Four Nations Tournament in Scarborough would take some beating.

However, it is the success of the FA Vase competition which has given me most satisfaction. Introduced after the abolition of amateur status, it immediately provided a very real chance of a Wembley appearance for thousands of players and officials who could previously have only dreamt of it. It is a pleasure many years to meet ex-players who still treasure memories of a very special day. I also recall going into the West End to buy the Vase itself!

Amongst my hopes for the future would be that, despite the obvious opportunity of progress offered by the National League System, clubs will realistically assess their own particular ability to play at a higher level and not jeopardise their long-term future for the sake of fleeting glory. Too many famous old clubs have paid a costly penalty for overstretching themselves.

Adrian Titcombe

MARTIN TYLER still coaches at non-league clubs when he has time from his career as one of the world's leading football commentators with Sky and enjoyed his playing days with Corinthian-Casuals and his special club Woking.

My greatest experience of non-League football is on going, that of simply being involved.

It started with following my beloved Woking, with the highlights of watching Wembley wins in the old Amateur Cup in 1958 and the Geoff Chapple hat-trick of triumphs in the FA Trophy in the 1990's.

I also particularly cherish being given a game for Woking Reserves on one personally wonderful evening in 2004.

The fellowship I enjoyed at Corinthian Casuals in my more youthful playing days was second to none. More recently when work commitments have allowed I've been pleased to be an extra pair of hands for Alan Dowson during his spell as manager of Walton and Hersham. Last January I followed him to Kingstonian and I now have first hand knowledge of how competitive the non-league game is these days even in the Ryman Division One South.

As a television commentator I have been lucky enough to travel all over the football map. No other nation has a pyramid structure such as ours. We should be very proud of it.

Martin Tyler

BARRY FRY was a schoolboy international whose playing career has been overshadowed by his effervescent style of managership at Barnet and Birmingham City, where he was never short of publicity, and his whole hearted love affair with Peterborough United to whom he has attracted a regular flow of non league talent.

I have been very lucky to spend over 25 years in Non League football both as a player and manager. I played for Romford, Bedford, St Albans and Stevenage and managed Dunstable and Barnet who I took into the football league after finishing second three times in the conference, and have had FA Cup giant killing results.

I was also honoured by the FA who appointed me manager of their FA XI on a couple of occasions.

To me the people who run Non League football clubs are the salt of the earth. They give their time, effort and money because they love the game and to me they are the UNSUNG HEROES.

Non League Football has improved beyond recognition and the talent that has come out of Non League football is second to none. Every club knows that if you buy a Non League player you will get 100% passion and commitment because they are hungry for success.

The atmosphere, spirit and quality of Non League is clear for everyone to see and I congratulate Tony Williams and thank him on behalf of the millions of Non League lovers for his magnificent contribution over the last 30 years.

Barry Fry

BRYAN MOORE was the Chairman of Yeovil Town who masterminded the survival of the club when a previous regime had left it near to collapse. He has been a dedicated F.A. councillor and given great service to the non-league game.

For the past 60 years I have had the privilege and pleasure of playing, watching and administering the wonderful game of football. During this time I have experienced many highs and lows. My best times however, have been in non-league.

The first low and a huge shock was when Street beat Yeovil in the F.A. Cup in 1947. This was followed by a real high when Yeovil beat the mighty Sunderland 2-1 in the Fourth Round of the F.A. Cup in February 1949.

Another high spot came and, once more, it was the F.A. Cup that provided it. The night of the 16th December 1992 will live forever in my memory. It was the night Yeovil beat Hereford United in the second round replay. Yes Yeovil had gone much further than this in the competition many times in the past, but what was good about this night was that the winners were to entertain the mighty Arsenal in the next round. At that time Yeovil were in dire financial straits and the small board of directors, which included Tony Williams, and the wonderful supporters were fighting desperately to keep the club afloat. Receipts from that game did not solve the problem, but it helped a lot and also gave everyone the strength to carry on the fight.

In 1944 I was elected to serve on the F.A. Council, a very proud moment for me indeed. This was followed up in May 2002 when Yeovil, at last reached the F.A. Trophy final. For me, not only was that very special but also I was the chairman of the F.A. Trophy Committee at the time so had the thrill of walking out to meet my team before the game. An even bigger thrill followed at the end of the game when I went onto the pitch to present the victorious Yeovil team with their medals.

I have been privileged to meet many people during my time and have many friends in the game throughout the country. The spirit and standard of non-league football has never been stronger, both on and off the pitch, and I am sure it will go from strength to strength.

Brian Moore

RON TARRY is an example of one of the loyal football lovers who serve local clubs all over the country and he is still working hard for his beloved Hungerford Town after sixty years service in just about every role.

Non-league football received a terrific boost when the F.A. Trophy and F.A. Vase returned to Wembley, this time to the long-awaited new National Stadium where all four teams put on displays, which shamed our two top Premiership clubs Manchester United and Chelsea, and my love of football at this level was vindicated.

The whole of my career of more years than I care to mention has been connected with my home town of Hungerford, and, when Tony Williams moved into the area all those years ago and became involved with the club, we took an immense step foward.

The England team trained on the pitch, we entertained Kuwait and Saudi Arabia, represented England in the Anglo-Italian Cup, and saw many celebrities all thanks to him, although we never rose higher than the Isthmian League Division 2, and were beaten in three F.A. Vase Semi-Finals, after being runners-up four times in the Berks. & Bucks Senior Cup, we finally beat the mighty Wycombe Wanderers in the final.

For 30 years the Non-League Directory and its predecessors have recorded the ups and downs of every club in the country, and Tony Williams was there to remind us all of our duty to the game.

With the Premiership moving farther and farther away from the average fan, it behoves us all to ensure that non-league football remains a game that we can all continue to enjoy, whatever our level in the pyramid.

Ron Tarry

ALAN SMITH has become a highly respected football correspondant for the Daily Telegraph and Sky Television since a magnificent career in which he became one of just three players who represented England at full and Non-League levels

Without non-league football, I would never have been able to break into the pro-ranks.

For me, the club in question was Alvechurch FC, a village team in essence but one that has forged a fantastic reputation in non-league circles. What a great bunch of lads. What a fantastic experience, the highlight being when I won international honours with the England semi-pro side.

I'll always look back on my time at Alvechurch with tremendous affection, as I do at non-league football in general. It remains an extremely important level of the game. We should never forget that.

Alan Smith

BRIAN WAKEFIELD is a dedicated football man who was a quality goalkeeper who played at every level from the Great Britain Olympic squad, through senior non-league football to the Corinthian-Casuals side that promotes football in schools across the country.

I was lucky enough to have played top amateur football prior to the abolition of the distinction between amateurs and professionals in 1974. Although this was an eternity ago, memories are still vivid and many friendships remain.

My Isthmian League debut was for Corinthian Casuals against Barking in August 1959. Tony Williams scored twice in a 4-1 win and we have been friends ever since. I hope that those playing today get as much fulfilment from the game as myself.

Although the F.A.Trophy and F.A.Vase Finals do not attract the same crowds as the F.A. Amateur Cup Finals (100,000 on five occasions!) and a non-league international match does not have the same ring as the old Amateur International, there has been an immense growth in the popularity and standard of non-league football at every level.

I have attended both this year's Trophy final and the F.A.Cup Final, although the skill level was obviously higher in the latter, but there was greater commitment and passion in the former and this made it the better spectacle.

A major contributory factor in generating and maintaining public interest in non-league football has been through the endeavours of Tony, whose enthusiasm for the game is unbounded. Non-League football owes him a great deal and he is to be congratulated on producing the thirtieth edition of the Non-League Club Directory
Brian Wakefield

Barry Bright is a Vice Chairman of The Football Association and Chairman of the F.A. Disciplinary Committee who is also a great supporter of non-league football in Kent.

The wonderful 30th birthday of the bible of Non-League football coincides with the first year of a restructured Football Association Council.

After many years of canvassing for representation, the opportunity of a direct voice in the F.A.Council Chamber for Non-League football is achieved - may it be used with wisdom by those entrusted on behalf of their respective leagues to the overall benefit of the great family of football.

Barry Bright

GORDON TAYLOR enjoyed a long Football League career and is now giving great service to the game as Chairman of the Professional Footballers Association.

It is an honour and privelige to be asked by Tony Williams to contribute to the special 30th edition of the non-League Club Directory especially in this the centenary year of the PFA.

It has been a pleasure in this centenary year to look at the history of the professional game and appreciate the strong base of our football pyramid that is unique in the world. One of the most satisfying moments of my career was to be part of the Heathrow Football League agreement in the mid 80's when the bigger clubs in Division One were looking to keep more of the television monies and I was part of the committee that introduced the play-offs having experienced them at first hand whilst playing for Vancouver Whitecaps in 1977 in the NASL. Not only have the play-offs been an exciting introduction to the game creating interest throughout all divisions, but on that day we introduced automatic promotion from outside the Football League for the very first time, initially starting with one and of course now having both automatic promotion and a play-off place.

My next door neighbour is a Morecambe supporter and rather like Andy Warhol's famous quotation - that every club, like every individual, can have their moment in the sun - and that arrived with their magnificent play-off victory over Exeter and as he likes to remind me Morecambe played at the new Wembley before the likes of Liverpool! Not only that, his face is captured in the crowd by the club photographer during Morecambe's winning goal.

It is very satisfying that in spite of the doom and gloom predicted with the disproportionate amount of money going to the Premier League, the Conference clubs have 50 per cent of their players employed on a full-time basis and the quality of football outside the Premier League and the Football League is there for all to see by the success of promoted teams. Accrington Stanley set a marvellous example in coming back into the league after their virtual extinction in the early 60's. I also have to say that the club I started with, Hurst Wesleyans that became Curzon Ashton, nearly made it to the new Wembley, but were rather thwarted by the excellent Truro team in the FA Vase.

The Non-league game continues to thrive as evidenced by the quality of football at the F.A. Trophy and Vase finals and the Conference Play-off. May you all continue to enjoy the excellent Non-League Paper and The Non-League Club Directory keeping in touch in a most informative way with your fellow football lovers at the very grass roots level of the game, continuing to make our game the greatest in the world, enjoyed by spectators and participants alike. My heartiest congratulations on your 30th birthday edition. *Gordon Taylor*

Non-League Newspaper

Non-League football covers at least 95% of our most popular national winter sport in this country and featuring it superbly every week end throughout the year, is The Non-League Paper.

The publication was an exciting inspirational brain child of David Emery, an experienced Fleet Street journalist, who built an editorial team to provide Non-League's special weekly publication which was launched at the beginning of the century.

The Non-League Paper has provided wonderful coverage of football competitions below Football League level with an excellent team of journalists, who understand the respect and loyalty given to Non-League football throughout the country.

Now in charge as Editor in Chief, David has encouraged his company to publish a variety of sporting publications, in which The Non-League Paper has been edited by Stuart Hammonds and Alex Narey.

2007 - 2008

Two of my favourite Non-League memories take me back to this campaign. The Non-League FA Cup runs are always special, but this year the Havant & Waterlooville story boarded on the unbelievable. I caught up with 'The Hawks' after they had beaten Bognor Regis Town 2-1 (a), Fleet Town 2-1 (h) and Leighton Town 3-0 (h) and had claimed the Football League scalps of York City 1-0 (a) and Notts Co 1-0 (a).

I travelled to The Liberty Stadium, Swansea's lovely new ground and enjoyed an excellent cup tie which produced a 1-1 draw. The replay was televised and both teams obviously knew the winners would be travelling to Anfield in the Fourth Round. Another thrilling cup tie attracted 4,000 to The Beveree Stadium and a 4-2 home victory sent the whole of Hampshire into FA Cup delirium.

I had always had a soft spot for Liverpool since I realised that their famous World Cup winner Roger Hunt and I had played together for the FA XI against London University and we had remained friends ever since.

So a trip to Anfield to see a Non-League club competing with famous Liverpool in the FA Cup was a dream come true. Massive support travelled up from Hampshire to help the attendance reach an impressive 42,566, one suspected there were a few on loan from Portsmouth, but the away support made themselves heard.

As usual, the Kop welcomed their humble visitors with polite scouse humour and everyone involved with 'The Hawks' just glowed, as they enjoyed the thrill of contributing to the atmosphere in a packed Anfield Stadium. The teams came out and we had to pinch ourselves again to realise little Havant & Waterlooviille were actually about to take on the famous Liverpool. Everyone new ' They would Never Walk Alone' and 'hope was in their hearts' as many a tear and a goosebump appeared on the toughest football fan.

If we thought this was the very best a Non-League supporters could experience, we were very quickly lifted up onto another even more delirious platform, as Richard Pacquette scored for the visitors after just eight minutes.

Of course Liverpool equalised and we thought the underdogs' moments of glory were probably all over. But no, Alfie Potter scored after half an hour and once again the Kop atmosphere was quietly respectful. When Liverpool equalised before half time we all realised we had probably seen the end of the Non-League heroics and a final 4-2 home victory was well deserved. Our wonderful Non-League cup day would be remembered by everyone present for the rest of their lives. It was made even more memorable by the sporting and amusing atmosphere created by the character of the local fans.

At the other end of the season, we were all paying tributes to the achievements of Kirkham & Wesham of The North West Counties Division One, a club who were making their debut in the FA Vase. If written as a fairy story it probably wouldn't have been believed. This little club, making it's competition debut, played twelve FA Vase games and won the Final thanks to two goals from a seventeen year old reserve Matt Walwyn, who came on with his club 0-1 down and just eight minutes to go. Kirkham & Wesham became AFC Fylde for 2008-2009 and have continued to progress!

Looking at the Conference final table that season, the ex League clubs were challenging for a return, with Aldershot Town way ahead of Cambridge United, Torquay United and Exeter City but Burton Albion were getting stronger every year and Histon had enjoyed their best season in their history.

'England C' once again competed in 'The International Challenge Trophy' over two years, with an Under 23 squad and their full England Non-League squad in the Four Nations Tournament where Gibraltar replaces Ireland.

Manager Paul Fairclough and his assistant Steve Burr were proving a great success and with administration handled with genuine care by Mike Appleby at The Football Association. This was a very happy and successful England squad. So it was no surprise that England C remained unbeaten in both competitions and only conceded two goals in seven internationals.

My season was much the same, touring the West Country, following the FA's cup competitions and keeping an eye on the Islands competing with the English League representative sides. I was also pleased to see The Royal Air Force winning the inter services without conceding a goal and the wonderful new Coventry City ground hosted the F.A. National League System Cup Final won on penalties by The Southern Amateur League who beat The Midland Football Combination.

Mike was doing tremendous work producing 1168 pages for the Directory and I enjoyed keeping the week to week club records. Although there was now no magazine to work on, it was good to see David Emery's Non-League Paper giving the game such excellent service and we felt our level of the game was being well promoted.

2007 - 2008

Teamsheet

The FA Cup, 4th Round – Sponsored by e.on
LIVERPOOL v HAVANT & WATERLOOVILLE
Saturday 26th January 2008

Liverpool
(Red Shirts)

30	Charles Itandje
3	Steve Finnan
4	Sami Hyypia (c)
6	John Arne Riise
11	Yossi Benayoun
15	Peter Crouch
16	Jermaine Pennant
19	Ryan Babel
20	Javier Mascherano
21	Lucas
37	Martin Skrtel

Havant & Waterlooville
(Yellow Shirts)

1	Kevin Scriven
2	Jay Smith
3	Phil Warner
4	Shaun Wilkinson
5	Tom Jordan
6	Neil Sharp
7	Mo Harkin
8	Jamie Collins (c)
9	Richard Pacquette
10	Rocky Baptiste
11	Alfie Potter

Substitutes

40	David Martin
8	Steven Gerrard
9	Fernando Torres
18	Dirk Kuyt
23	Jamie Carragher

Substitutes

12	Jamie Slabber
14	Charlie Oatway
15	Tony Taggart
16	Steven Gregory
17	Tom Taylor

Referee
P Dowd

Assistant Referees
G M Brittain & R Burton

4th Official
L S Mason

 Liverpool Football Club extend a warm welcome to our visitors for today's match at Anfield
www.liverpoolfc.tv

2008 - 2009

The highlight of this season was undoubtedly the involvement of eight Non-League clubs in the Third Round Proper of the FA Challenge Cup. Of the eight, only Kidderminster Harriers failed to claim a Football League scalp that season, but of course the Harriers have enjoyed many cup triumphs in the past.

F.A. Cup Giant Killing

Blyth Spartans	3-1 v	Shrewsbury T. (h)
(Conf North)	0-0 v	Bournemouth (a)
	1-0 v	Bournemouth (h)
Histon	1-0 v	Swindon Town (h)
(Conference)	1-0 v	Leeds United (a)
Kettering Town	1-1 v	Lincoln City (h)
(Conference)	2-1 v	Lincoln City (a)
	1-1 v	Notts County (a)
	2-1 v	Notts County (h)
Barrow (Conference)	2-1 v	Brentford (h)
Eastwood T (N.P.L)	2-0 v	Wycombe W. (h)
Forest Green R (Conf)	2-0 v	Rochdale (h)
Torquay United (Conf)	1-0 v	Blackpool (h)

Conference Premier clubs joined the FA Cup for the Fourth Qualifying Round but Blyth Spartan supporters had eight FA Cup ties to enjoy and Eastwood Town nine.

The final Conference table showed Histon in third place, a record for the little Cambridge club, and it was good to see AFC Wimbledon making their way up to the top level as Conference South champions. Alfreton Town and Eastleigh were also showing their ambitions in promising seasons in Conference North and South respectively.

For nine years, James Wright an old friend and dedicated Non-League enthusiast, had been producing 'Non-League Newsdesk', an excellent publication, as a pre-season handbook. James had realised it had become impossible to complete the book in time, thanks mainly to the fact that Step Five clubs started their season at the end of the first week in August. So he suggested a merger with our Directory which Mike and I were pleased to accept.

The new 2010 Directory once again filled 1168 pages with James concentrating on statistical elements of Step Five and Six and all of Step Seven downwards.

The FA National Systems Cup kicked off again as a two season competition and in The Preliminary Round Guernsey produced a shock 6-0 victory over The Kent County League Jersey beat the Spartan South Midlands and The Isle of Man beat The Manchester League 1-0. The Islands were really enjoying the competition and perhaps as they were all drawn at home in this round, their visitors might have been 'relaxing' too much in the holiday atmosphere!

The previous competition winners 'The Southern Amateur League were placed in Qualifying Group Two with CR Piemonte Valle DAosta' (Italy), 'Region 1' (Republic of Ireland) and East Of Scotland (Scotland).

Despite a better goal difference than the Italians, the English representatives were placed third in their final table. Perhaps it was judged on goals scored.

Since the abolishing of The Amateur Internationals we had consistently promoted the idea that Non-League footballers should have the opportunity to represent their country as the 'best players at their particular level of the game'.

This season the subject was highlighted again, as senior clubs were still unhappy about losing their players for representative games during the season. Paul Fairclough and his excellent team had seen their selections enjoy an unbeaten run but testing friendlies were needed before we faced Italy needing a point to qualify for the FInal of the European Tournament.

So a fixture was arranged with a very strong Boznia Herzegovina B side who contained Under 21 and full internationals. Although losing 2-6 the trip away helped the bonding and the squad were ready to travel to Italy where a thrilling 2-2 draw earned England C a home final against Belgium. One more 'friendly' was won 4-0 in Malta and the Final v Belgium was to be played at The Kassam Stadium, home of Oxford United who were competing in the Conference at the time.

An official dinner at the historic Oriel College in Oxford University, was appreciated by all involved, and the fine work of the management team was recognised as an important development in Non-League football.

On the day, the experienced Belgians proved just too strong and won 1-0. The season had provided an exciting, enjoyable but inconsistent programme for Non-League International players. The general hope was for The Football Association to introduce a senior England Non-League XI, being the best players with clubs outside the Football League, and an England C squad for younger players.

2009 - 2010

With James Wright and Craig Pottage, a great football statistician joining the editorial team I concentrated on another season based on South Western clubs, especially in the FA competitions. There was an introduction to Futsal tournaments which displayed commendable indoor skills and Channel Islands football was given excellent publicity throughout the campaign.

My special favourites from Guernsey enjoyed their best ever season in The FA Carlsberg National League System. Competing against the mainland leagues gave the Islanders valuable experience and I enjoyed visits this season to see them beat 'The Southern Amateur League, The Hertfordshire Senior Amateur County League and The Dorset Premier Football League.

These successes took them into The Final against The Liverpool County Premier League with the knowledge that the Winners would be invited to represent England in 'The UEFA Regions Cup. The final proved a wonderful boost to Channel Island football as Guernsey won with an impressive 5-2 victory.

Another interesting link with the Channel Islands was the introduction of The Clydesdale Bank International Tournament played in Guernsey. The Bank were also sponsoring the Scottish Football League and two of their members, Hamilton Academicals and Motherwell, joined Guernsey Athletics and Jersey Scottish in an original tournament played at the Island's excellent Footes Lane ground.

The pressure on the leading Conference clubs was increasing every season and this time Stevenage Borough managed brilliantly by Graham Westley, pulled well away from runners-up Luton Town by eleven points.

Crawley Town and AFC Wimbledon were making their presence felt in the Conference but some clubs were finding the pressure of keeping up with the leaders a great financial strain such as Kettering Town and Eastbourne Borough.

Salisbury City, Hayes & Yeading and Histon all finished in mid table showing signs of the pressure. Following their great results in the FA Cup in the previous season, the 2009-2010 competition put the Non-League clubs back in their place. Just three managed to reach The Third Round Proper this year and had no luck in the draw, Barrow, Forest Green Rovers and Luton Town all losing away from home.

England C continued their happy development and kicked off in another International Challenge Trophy with a 2-1 victory over the Republic of Ireland. They would also meet Wales and Estonia in the following season, hoping to reach another Cup Final.

Full marks to the Football Association who have introduced a 'RESPECT' campaign and hopefully it will be embraced by all levels of the game.

Club colours spread below from a series featured in Fairplay

2010 - 2011

The season started with an impressive Armed Forces Charity Day at Taunton Town and as the season developed it was confirmed that the new ambitious clubs in the Conference, Crawley Town and AFC Wimbledon, were indeed the ones who gained promotion to The Football League. Crawley as Champions, plus Wimbledon who beat Luton Town in the play-offs after penalties at Manchester City's glorious new ground. Just imagine how costly that shoot out must have been!

As grounds all over the country are steadily improving, so too are the match day programmes, mostly varying from 28 to 56 pages and costing £1.50 to £2.50. From the grounds I visited, I was most impressed by Newport County, with a glossy colourful 40 pages at £2.80, Harrow Borough's FA Cup issue for their Chesterfield FA Cup tie, contained 56 pages costing £2.50 and little Sherborne Town provided a glossy fully coloured 28 page edition for just £1.00.

Congratulations to all those programme editors throughout the country who produce such enjoyable and useful match day magazines. Hopefully those with plenty of advertisements and regular sales will have made a well deserved profit from their programmes by the end of the season.

Once again England C enjoyed a successful and exciting season. A warm up friendly against Wales was drawn 2-2 and was followed by a 1-0 victory over Estonia in their qualifying group. This gave them the chance of revenge against Belgium who had beaten them in the previous Final.

Paul Fairclough, Steve Burr and their backroom team created a great atmosphere in which their youngsters are very well coached while preparing to face European countries fielding far more experienced players. So a 1-0 victory over the cup holders gave great satisfaction and the chance to compete in another final, this time against Portugal at Northampton Town's ground.

Sadly for the management who had done so much to promote England C, the final clashed with the Conference Promotion Play-Offs and eight of the squad involved with the Semi-Final were unavailable for the Final. After a very brave and encouraging performance against some very experienced Portugese players, the game was lost by the only goal of the game.

This was England C's third consecutive final, with a win followed by two defeats but the quality, attitude and general spirit of the youngsters has brought only credit upon the promising squads and their dedicated coaching team.

A bitter sweet experience was the sight of Charterhouse playing Eton in the schools cup final under the title of 'The Boodles ISFA Cup Final' at the lovely Milton Keynes Stadium. These schools were undoubtedly two of the pioneers of the game in this country, in fact they met in 1881 when their respective Old Boys teams contested the FA Cup Final !

The 'bitter' side to the occasion for me was the fact that in my playing days at Malvern and with the Old Malvernians, we had been considered one of the very strongest schools playing Association Football with a very successful Old Boys side. These successful teams had been coached by Denis Saunders, the captain of the famous Pegasus FA Amateur Cup winning sides, but after national acclaim and wonderful traditions as one of the best soccer playing schools. It was decided to play rugby, not football, in the Autumn term.

Old Malvernians had even won The FA Amateur Cup in 1902, beating Bishop Auckland 5-2, so the change would probably cut off our traditional schools football fixtures, leaving us as a second rate rugby school and sadly, a second rate football school which, for me, was heartbreaking!

The 'sweet' side to the occasion was the fact that captain of the winning Charterhouse side was Jack Ryder-Smith, son of the skipper in our most successful Old Malvernian seasons.

Mike was working hard to compile the Directory and I enjoyed keeping the various statistics for leagues, clubs and players up to date from week to week throughout the season. Puma were good sponsors and the latest book was a mammoth 1136 pages.

We felt we were still providing the Non-League world with an annual, of which they could be proud. But we were originally providing the annual on behalf of the FA Chief Executive, Ted Croker, who was a real Football Man, having played League and Non-League football.

He had realised the competitions below the Football League featuring 95% of the game in this country under the leadership of The FA, deserved their own annual. He then suggested we provided one with their blessing, and if necessary, their support. A little interest, help and support would always have been welcome.

2011 - 2012

The main feature of a Non-League season now centres around the battle for promotion to the Football League. The Conference was becoming equally split between ex League clubs desperate to return and the Non-League clubs determined to achieve their ambitions for League Football. The Conference Champions were Fleetwood Town, a club that had stormed up the Non-League pyramid and had become impressive champions by five points, while they were joined in promotion by ex League club York City who had shaken off the challenge of Luton Town, Mansfield Town and Wrexham.

Sadly for the prestige of Non-League football's senior knock-out cup competition, The FA Trophy tended to be overshadowed by the promotion race, as far as the senior Non-League clubs were concerned. But York City managed their season brilliantly, they hung on in the Conference top five, while also earning a Wembley Final against lowly Newport County, which they won. Promotion was also achieved by beating Luton Town 2-1 in a second Wembley success.

To reach The FA Cup Second Round was an exciting achievement for Non-League clubs Grimsby Town and Gateshead, but to be drawn against Non-League colleagues was a real disappointment. Salisbury City beat Grimsby Town away and then lost to Sheffield United, while Tamworth won at Gateshead before losing in the Third Round after a thrilling afternoon at Everton.

Fleetwood had an incredible reward for reaching the Third Round by being drawn at home for a 'local derby' with Blackpool. In the seasons to come, Fleetwood were to overtake their famous neighbours, but on this occasion they lost 1-5, in front of 5,092.

Watching Fleetwood in their FA Cup replay at Yeovil, who were now missing their reputation as an FA Cup team to be avoided, the exchange of reputations was very obvious. The Non-League club enjoying the lack of pressure and great Conference results, faced a lowly Football League club with nothing to gain and the dread of the home supporters quite obviously affecting the Yeovil players, many of whom had no idea of their club's previous romantic FA Cup reputation. The result: Yeovil Town 0 Fleetwood 2.

Our Non-League Club Directory included a thorough record of the England C results with cap winners and scorers plus a complete review of England International Cap winning players, including England Semi-Professionals, National Game XI and England C.

However, our lads hadn't enjoyed their usual winning start to an International Challenge Trophy campaign. A warm up fixture in Gibralter was lost and a battling 1-1 draw in a trophy match at home to Italy was followed by a disappointing 0-4 defeat in Russia.

The most worrying aspect of the modern Non-League game, through the eyes of someone who has seen it develop over the last forty years, is the incredible increase in Referees issuing more and more yellow and red cards. Hardly a tackle or a mere challenge can be made without at least a free kick and often a 'card'. Competitive spirit can quickly disappear from the game as players are careful not to get sent off with a second card or indeed as has happened, for a team to be reduced to eight or nine players.

The game has not become any dirtier and if referees really concentrated on punishing 'intent' instead of clumsiness or (as in many Non-League games) a basic lack of skill, the modern game would enjoy a much more honest reputation.

Enter the Gladiators, the fans have been waiting for this moment 'here come the heroes' Players tunnels were much smaller than they are today.

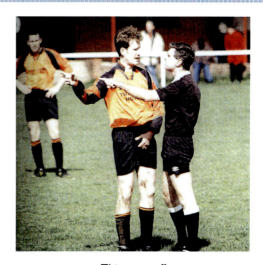

This way ref?

2012 - 2013

Looking back over the editorials in The Non-League Club Directory, it is quite obvious that the general attitude throughout the national game of Association Football has been changing much to the disappointment of the older fans.

The depressing news in the national press this year was the fact that following the Olympic Games, which we hoped would inspire the nation, the numbers involved in all sports throughout the country had dropped, with Association Football being the sport which had been hit by the biggest drop.

Michael, as general manager of Loddiswell in local South Devon football was finding it more and more difficult to field two sides each week end. Young players just were not kicking a ball about when they had exciting technology with which to enjoy their spare time.

In senior Non-League football, promotion and progress up the ladder had become very important and to achieve this, management of clubs all over the country would be attracting better players to take the place of locals. Better payments would be offered to attract these new signings, but unless there was an immediate improvement in quality, the local supporters would be less enthusiastic to watch new players who they felt had no obvious loyalty to 'their club' and were possibly just there to pick up the money.

For every club that benefits by increasing payments to attract outside talent, four or five clubs have been seen to struggle financially by stretching their finances. Some clubs have closed down, others have started again with changed names or may have dropped down the local pyramid to rebuild.

Of course we have seen and admired success stories such as Burton Albion, Fleetwood, and Crawley Town while AFC Wimbledon and Dagenham & Redbridge have come through difficulties to move steadily forward.

This season the promotion race to the Football League was dominated by League 'Old Boys' with Mansfield Town, ahead of runners-up Kidderminster Harriers by two points. Newport County winning the play-offs also contested by Grimsby Town and Wrexham.

Paul Fairclough started the season with the experience of 50 England Internationals behind him, which was nearly as many games as had been enjoyed by all six previous managers together. But the England C team faced strong competition in The International Challenge Trophy. They won 2-1 in Belgium but lost 0-1 at home to Turkey, which meant they would not be competing in the Final for the first time in four years - an impressive record!

Once the ground has been prepared it should be perfect

What is he thinking?

Clear unambiguous signs are important

Just checking everything's in the right position goalie

You Have to Love it

Everyone gets settled in, although some spectators appear to need a bit of assistance - coming in or going out?

Could confuse a simple fellow

But the excitement sometimes gets too much

The photos in 'You Have to Love it' are great fun and have been sent by our excellent team of photographers who have helped us with our books for many years.

If anyone has taken amusing photos at Non-League grounds, please send them to:
t.williams320@btinternet.com
and if we include them in the Next Non-League Directory we will send you a free copy.

This is the way to take a free kick.

Conclusion 2017

Living in Somerset really reduced the opportunities to cover the national leagues throughout the huge Non-League world. So once my loyalty to Yeovil Town was no longer a priority, I relaxed and enjoyed visiting clubs throughout the West of England while concentrating on the FA knock out competitions for the Cup, Trophy and Vase.

I had enjoyed watching younger son John with his games for Kingsbridge and Mike's involvement with Loddiswell and North Curry, while a visit to Tiverton Town was one of my most enjoyable outings and 'Tivvy' was just down the M5 from Taunton.

The character of the Non-League world was changing. Quite naturally, money became more important, as club chairmen desperately tried to find ways in which they could outbid their rivals for the signature of the best local players, or perhaps for players who needed even more money to persuade them to travel.

Consequently, footballers became greedier and many players, with limited talent, were also jumping on the bandwagon to take advantage of the competitive clubs, who were desperate for promotion to senior leagues. Managers were realizing they had to achieve the chairman's target for success and they were not likely to get very long to prove themselves. So for some, standards of sportsmanship and respect for the game were put on one side, success had to be achieved at all costs. For the older supporters, who had probably been in love with the game, its principles and spirit all their lives, this general change of attitude hurt. Money and consequently winning at all costs, became the main aims for many clubs and their staff on and off the field.

Habits were changing for some of the traditional happy go lucky local clubs. where a hard core of local players had become friends of the supporters in a cheerful clubhouse, enjoying their Saturdays home or away together, win or lose.

Many of the players travelling to earn their generous weekly money, would no longer stay for long to socialise with club members in the club house, as they had to drive home. General spirit on and off the field was changing, but many clubs were improving and many players were of a higher standard and often good to watch.

In general, senior Non-League football was becoming more professional, but some clubs just could not, or did not wish to, keep up with the ever increasing payments to players, for transfer fees or for improving their facilities. If you look back over the present century, you will note that some clubs have disbanded, some closed down and perhaps re-formed with a new name while others have blossomed into successful fully professional clubs.

International Change of Character

Some ambitious chairmen of senior Non-League clubs made it quite clear that they didn't want their best players taken away during the season to play representative football, even if they were playing for their country and bringing good publicity to their clubs.

The traditional England v Scotland Amateur or Semi-Professional internationals, the home nations semi-professional championship or even the Inter-League Representative competitions that had been enjoyed all over the country, just did not suit the club chairmen. They wanted their best players, who they were paying, to be available for their clubs and their clubs alone. This attitude was quite understandable, but some great competitions, wonderful friendships and exciting experiences on and off the field, had provided the players, officials and loyal fans with some great occasions and wonderful memories which have been missed by the older supporters.

To be picked for the England team representing the massive Non-League world, was an impressive honour and it was good for England fans to see an international squad representing the very best players within our levels of the game.

So the Non-League world has been changing. It was great news for the game when The Football League clubs accepted promotion for the top Non-League club in 1987 and, since 2003, the life changing step up was made available for two clubs every year. The introduction of a super league at the top of the Non-League pyramid in 1979 was the start of a new challenge to the whole of Non-League football.

The original 20 clubs (13 from The Southern League and 7 from the North Premier League) earned their places in the new exciting competition through their league positions in the 1978-1979 season. Leaving more places that could be earned, possibly by the famous Isthmian clubs.

The cream of the Northern Premier and Southern Leagues included some Non-League 'giants' . Well supported clubs such as Altrincham, Barnet, Boston United, Scarborough, Telford United, Weymouth and Yeovil Town were all well known names throughout the football world thanks to their exciting FA Cup performances. Of these pioneers, only Barrow are competing in Non-League football's senior competition in 2017, but 'The Blue Birds' had already enjoyed a long run as a Football League club before the Conference was launched.

If you respect the game you love and are proud of your sport's principles of fair play and sportsmanship, every incident of deliberate cheating is sickening to see and of course does no good at all to the spirit and image of 'our national game'. I'm proud of football and hate to see trends creeping in that will bring the modern game and its image into disrepute.

Conclusion 2017

Hopefully, improvements to football are considered regularly by the game's administrators. So, if they seriously care for the national sport, we will be able to enjoy a more honest, but still competitive game in the seasons ahead.

Michael and I have been lucky to have been involved with Non-League football all our lives and although we hear, and sometimes agree, that times are changing. Just think of the improvements we have seen over the years.

Forty years is a long time in the football world. So looking back through our publications which also included a variety of magazines promoting all levels of the game, there is no doubt the whole Non-League football world and its principles have changed.

A worrying change in attitudes can be seen. If a strong tackle hurt you I was taught as a young player- never give your opponent satisfaction by showing him you are hurt or injured.

They Loved their Football at The FA

However, after a tackle these days, we now regularly see the modern tactic which can include a squeal, falling theatrically and thumping the ground in absolute agony! In fact doing everything possible to get an opponent into trouble by winning a free kick and possibly encouraging the referee to issue a red or yellow card.

But let's concentrate on the positives:

* The club facilities have never been better

* Playing surfaces have improved at all levels.

* General fitness has improved thanks to the club facilities and financial incentives.

* The FA Trophy and FA Vase finals day still gives Non-League clubs and their supporters the chance of a special Wembley experience.

* The best Non-League clubs can progress into the Football League.

* The regional and national pyramids of leagues give successful clubs a chance to progress on and off the field. Financial incentives at all levels have never been so exciting in the history of the game

---

Do the players, club officials and supporters really feel satisfaction from a victory through cheating?

It's been a privilege to have been involved in a game I have loved all my life. It has given me some wonderful memories, great friends and a great deal of satisfaction and I can only hope that many more people will enjoy equally happy lives within the modern game in the future.

For the last forty years we have enjoyed producing an annual in which we have attempted to report on the previous year's competitions and to promote all that we admired within the Non-League game. We also enjoyed producing over a hundred 'Team Talks', a Non-League Monthly Football magazine, plus over twenty other football publications.

Originally The Football Association, with leaders such as Ted Croker and Graham Kelly, encouraged us to develop the Non-League publications, that covered 95% of the nation's football under the Football Association's jurisdiction.

Since the 1977-1978 edition of our Non-League annual we have had wonderful support from Steve Clark, Mike Appleby, Adrian Titcombe, Alan Odell and David Barber at The Football Association with Jack Pearce, Mark Harris, Brian Lee, Dennis Strudwick and Barry Bright particularly supportive senior football executives.

All these dedicated football people really cared about 'their game' and originally the vast majority of those working with them at the Football Association were proud to be involved at Lancaster Gate and Soho Square. They considered it an honour, enjoyed and treasured by the executives who promoted and cared for the game to which they were dedicated.

With twice as many staff now employed at Wembley Stadium and the massive money involved in football, it isn't surprising that the sheer dedication and love of the game has been overtaken by the need to be financially successful. The changing face of sport can also be traced in our national Rugby Union and Cricket headquarters in a similar fashion.

I have always been impressed with the way that everyone involved with Rugby League, their players, club officials, television commentators and the media, all promote their sport with an impressive loyalty and respect.

That 'old fashioned' love of their sport creates an atmosphere similar to the one in which I grew up, where football people loved and promoted all that was good in their game and tried to protect it from criticism. The Football Association was quite rightly the English game's strongest ally, promoting and protecting their game. Is that the case to-day? Hopefully it is!

Conclusion 2017

Some of the most enjoyable days for me have been when invited by Steve Clark, from The Competitions Department of the Football Association, to attend the FA Trophy and FA Vase Finals at Wembley Stadium.

The lunch at these wonderful Non-League occasions brings together many real Non-League workers who love the game and have promoted the competitions throughout the season.

Since 1978 we have attempted to promote Non-League football through our publications and have appreciated the co-operation, encouragement and help from The Football Association, originally by Ted Croker and Adrian Titcombe, and then Mike Appleby, David Barber, Steve Clark and Graham Noakes.

Over the last 50 years general principles and standards in the game have obviously changed on and off the field, and it is very easy to criticise the pressures that the massive increase in money has created.

But some uplifting games of football at vastly different levels recently reaffirmed that the game could still be played very competitively but also within a sporting spirit. England's Women and Youth sides provided some great television viewing and some wonderful. FA Cup ties featuring Leatherhead, Billericay Town, Manchester City and Bristol City all proved that the wonderful game was still alive and very special.

All these important games were thrilling and were contested in a determined but sporting atmosphere, that was so good for the game in general and also provided an example to all football lovers of how out wonderful game should be played and presented.

Michael has worked incredibly hard to keep the book 'alive.' His dedication to the game is immense but sadly he has had to battle at a time when books have become less popular, and Non-League football is not exactly fashionable. The original encouragement and support from the higher ranks at The Football Association is no longer apparent, so he has had an uphill battle to get the book printed each year.

I am extremely proud of him and the efforts he has put in to carry on promoting the original version of football with which he grew up. Sadly the attitudes within many aspects of football have changed in a way that is very difficult to respect. I hope that Michael and others with a sincere love of the game will at least enjoy their involvement and will continue to promote 'all that is good in football'.

Tony Williams
March 2018

'You Have to Love it '

This is a special book which illustrates all that is enjoyable about Non-League football. Our loyal team of photographers have enjoyed touring the Non-League grounds in all weathers, and their photographs illustrate Non-League football from avery 'angle'!

The action, atmosphere, determination, courage and possibly the most enjoyable of all, the humour of our wonderful game, is captured in this really enjoyable book of 176 pages which was published in 1996 selling at £14.99.

STILL AVAILABLE

I thought we had sold out but recently two old boxes were opened up to find we still had some books available in good condition. So they are available at £10 each (which includes postage and packing) from :
t.williams320@btinternet.com

Presented to Tony Williams
November 1986
For his continued promotion of all that is good in Football.

Photographers 2017

The Wembley Finals also give us a chance to thank all the enthusiastic and much appreciated photographers who send in photos and copy to Michael all season, in all weathers, without ever asking for or expecting payments. They love the game and they also enjoy the spirit in which they all work through the season meeting to work together at The Wonderful Wembley Stadium.

Thanks to: Peter Barnes, Graham Brown, Keith Clayton, Alan Coomes, Arthur Evans, Jonathon Hollaway, 'Uncle' Eric Marsh, Roger Turner, Bill Wheatcroft and Gordon Whittington.

A Selection of TW Publications

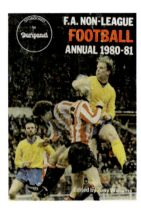
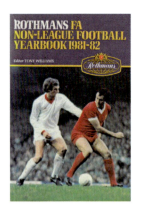
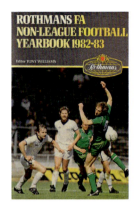
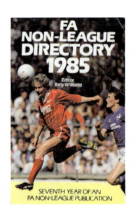
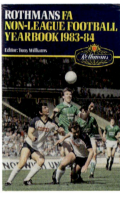

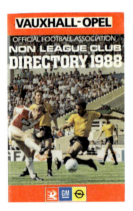

A Selection of TW Publications

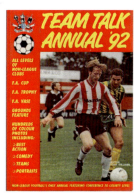

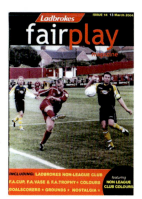
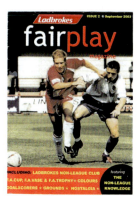

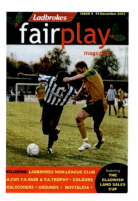

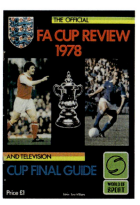

A Selection of TW Publications

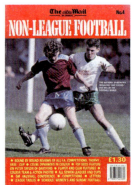

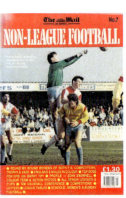